NTINI

A new coloured artistic guide

of

FLORENCE

and surroundings

EVERY USEFUL INFORMATION FOR THE TOURIST

100 coloured plates and the street
and monumental plan of the town

NOVA LVX

GIUSTI DI BECOCCI
Via Canto de' Nelli - Tel. 212478
FIRENZE

ITINERARIES-INDEX

2

ALPHABETICAL INDEX

HISTORICAL NOTE

The first traces of civilisation in the Arno Valley, where today the City of Florence stands, go back to the Villanovian period (Iron Age). The Etruscans ruled the district for many centuries till the Romans came and founded there a colony with the auspicious name of Florentia, in order to control and protect the important ford of the Arno.

During the period of the Middle Ages, the Colony was several times occupied and destroyed, but by about 1000 A.D. it had become a flourishing and prosperous little town, thanks above all to the wool trade. The building of the Baptistry, the first city's first architectural masterpiece, dates from this period. In the following centuries its increasing wealth, its intellectual and political ardour and the development and explosion within the city of violent passions and rivalries, made it the main and most fruitful nucleus of the peninsula's political life, and turned Florence into the cradle of the Renaissance and the centre of European civilisation.

It was a fief of the barons of Tuscany, amongst whome Matilda of Canossa was particularly outstanding at the time of the struggles for power between Pope Gregory VII and the Emperor Henry IV. Later it became the scene of fierce struggles between the old aristocracy and the powerful artisan class, organised in their guilds: this rivalry gave rise to the two factions of the Guelphs, who supported the Pope, and the Ghibellines, who supported the Emperor.

The fierce internal struggles did not however hamper the political, cultural and economic development of the city which, by the end of the 13th century, had extended its dominion over the rival cities of Siena, Arezzo and Pistoia, and was witnessing the creation of the masterpieces of Cimabue, Giotto, Dante and Arnolfo di Cambio. The literary works of Petrarca and Boccaccio bore eloquent testimony to the culture of Florence in the 14th century, together with the ornamental, half-Gothic architecture of Andrea di Cione, known by the name of Orcagna (1308-68). Meanwhile the city's political life, always in a state of ferment and agitation, erupted into the revolt of the populace against the « Magnati », i.e. the wealthy class, in the uprising of the « ciompi » (Woolcombers) in 1378, and saw the rising power of the great bankers, who were later to monopolise the city's life, and the flowering of the Dynasty of the Medici with Cosimo il Vecchio (1389-1464), a dynasty that was to preside over the city's destinies with varying fortune for some three centuries.

Cosimo was succeeded by his son, Piero il Gottoso (the Gouty, 1416-1469), and then by his grandson Lorenzo, known as the Magnificent (1449-1494), an artist and patron of the arts as well as a very shrewd politician, who brought Florence to its greatest splendour.

By now we have entered the period of full humanism: Man, the centre and measure of all things, is in search of those ideals of beauty, harmony and perfection, which in classical antiquity had carried him to the highest summits of art and knowledge, and it was in the ancient texts that he sought the fount of truth and the road to perfection.

In philosophy, the Platonism of Marsilio Ficino was dominant; in literature, the poetry of Poliziano and of Lorenzo the Magnificent was outstanding; in architecture, delicate sophistication gave place to the clear and serene conception of space of Brunelleschi (1377-1446), Michelozzo (1396-1472) and Rossellino (1427-1479); by the conquest of perspective, painting and sculpture freed themselves from any remaining traces of mysticism, and arrived at the full appreciation of the human personality and its setting. The greatest names in the history of art now emerge, such as Masaccio (1401-28), Beato Angelico (1387-1455), Paolo Uccello (1397-1475), Andrea del Castagno (1423-1457), Filippo Lippi (1406-1469), Sandro Botticelli (1444-1510), and in sculpture Donatello (1382-1466), Rosselino and Michelozzo.

The features that marked the artists of the 15th century reached their full development and their highest artistic values with the greatest exponents of Renaissance art: Michelangelo (1475-1564) and Leonardo (1452-1519).

Some years after Lorenzo's death, the Republican party, which was opposed to the « Signoria » and spurred on by the violently passionate preaching of the Dominican monk Gerolamo Savonarola, gained the upper hand and deluded itself into thinking that it could bring back the life of the city to its former purity of morals which, in the monk's view, had been defiled by luxury, the greed for gain und by an overwhelmingly prevailing worldly superficiality.

After their return, the Medici ruled, with a few interruptions, till 1737, when the dynasty died out with Giangastone.

Florence now became a Grand-Duchy and was ruled by the Austrian House of Lorraine which held it till, together with Tuscany, it was annexed to the Kingdom of Italy, whose capital it became in 1865.

From that time, the individual history of Florence merges with the wider horizon of Italian history.

FLORENCE TODAY

The City of the Flower and the Lily, as it is called from its coat of arms, is today a fairly large town with a population of about half a million.

Geographically, it is situated in that attractive area through which flows the river Arno (which Dante calls « the stream that rises in Falterona »), surrounded by the green, fertile hills which give it such a romantic setting, from the heights of Fiesole to Pratomagno and the Tuscan Apennines, and from the heights of Bellosguardo and Montacuto to the Chianti Hills.

Florence is not only a centre of industry, agriculture, trade and, above all, handicrafts, but also a very important centre of culture; let us suffice to mention here the University, the Cherubini Concervatory of Music, the Music Festivals (held at the Municipal and the Pergola Theatres, the Palazzo Pitti, the Hall of the Conservatory of Music and the Boboli Gardens), leaving aside all the other cultural manifestations.

Undoubtedly it is the artistic factor which makes Florence one of the most famous and important centres of tourism. Priceless treasures of every period and every style are preserved in its Museums, Churches and Palaces, so that by visiting them, we retrace in our minds the very path art has followed.

The terrible flood which struck it on November 4, 1966, seemed to have destroyed, in a few hours, a large part of that great inheritance, overwhelming and wiping out at the same time all the city's activities. The waters of the Arno reached a height of more than five metres at some points, submerging shops and houses, and sweeping away and destroying all their contents.

It likewise damaged, at times, alas! irreparably (as in the case of Cimabue's Crucifix), the works of art in the churches and the lower floors of the Galleries.

Those who come to Florence today do not notice the slightest sign of what happened, so fully has the life of the city been resumed in all its aspects, thanks to the efforts and the courage of its people. All one sees is a plaque on a wall, shop or house, recalling that disastrous day: « ON NOVEMBER 4, 1966, THE WATERS OF THE ARNO REACHED THIS HEIGHT '.

ITINERARY I

1) Piazza del Duomo and Piazza San Giovanni - 2) Baptistery of St. John the Baptist - 3) Cathedral of Santa Maria del Fiore - 4) Giotto's Campanile - 5) Loggia del Bigallo - 6) Museum « Opera del Duomo » - 7) Museum « Firenze com'era » (« Bygone Florence »)

BAPTISTRY AND CATHEDRAL

PIAZZA DEL DUOMO

Piazza del Duomo is not only the centre of the town and one of the most remarkable artistic monuments of Florence, but in addition and primarily the religious, most representative nucleus of the city.

The whole group of buildings, comprising the **Cathedral of Santa Maria del Fiore, Giotto's Campanile** and the **Baptistery of St. John the Baptist,** is generally called the Piazza del Duomo. More accurately, this name applies only to the two areas flanking the Cathedral: the area in front of the façade and including the Baptistry is known as the Piazza San Giovanni.

The traditional **« Scoppio del Carro »** (Blasting of the Cart) takes place in the Piazza del Duomo every year. The event, which was originated by a member of the Pazzi Family, who was present as a crusader at the capture of Jerusalem, is celebrated with a procession of members of the Town Council in historical costume. From the very ancient Church of the Holy Apostles, they carry the fire to the Cathedral. A large cart, drawn by picturesquely garlanded oxen and full of rockets and crackers, stops in front of the main door of the Cathedral, and a dove attached to a wire sets it on fire.

While the crackers explode with great noise, the bells of the city ring out in full peal. From the successful « course » of the dove, The Florentines see an omen for The new year.

This delightful event takes place on **Easter Sunday** morning.

THE BAPTISTERY

« Il mio bel San Giovanni », as Dante immortalised it in the Divine Comedy, was built on the remains of an old, early Christian Basilica in the 11th century and until 1128 was the ancient Cathedral of Florence.

EXTERIOR: The octagonal ground plan, the precise distribution of the volumes, the preference for a markedly geometrical pattern and the use of marble of two colours (white marble from Carrara and green serpentine from Prato), make this monument one of the most characteristic examples of Romanesque architecture in Tuscany.

The three bronze doors, arranged to correspond with three of the cardinal points, are of great artistic value.

SOUTH DOOR: This, the oldest of the three, was carved by **Andrea Pisano,** a pupil of Giotto, between 1330 and 1336. Divided into 28 panels, it depicts scenes from the life of St. John the Baptist and allegories representing the cardinal and theological virtues.

NORTH DOOR: Likewise divided into 28 panels, it is the work of **Lorenzo Ghiberti** who executed it in 1425 in collaboration with some of his pupils, among whom were **Donatello** and **Paolo Uccello.** They show scenes taken from the New Testament and from the lives of the Evangelists and the Doctors of the Church.

EAST DOOR: Michelangelo called this the **« Gate of Paradise »,** and it is **Lorenzo Ghiberti's** masterpiece: He took 27 years to complete it with the help of his son **Vittorio** and **Michelozzo** and **Benozzo Gozzoli.** The ten panels, covered with a patina of gold, represent scenes from the **Old Testament.**

The **« Gate of Paradise »** differs from the other two in three ways; it displays the narrative power so characteristic of Renaissance art; it has abandoned the Gothic line, so conspicuous in the previous doors and it applies the new rules of perspective, which Brunelleschi and Donatello had already experimented with, although less rigorously than these two artists.

SELF-PORTRAITS OF LORENZO AND VITTORIO GHIBERTI

BAPTISTERY - Porta del Paradiso - Interior mosaic

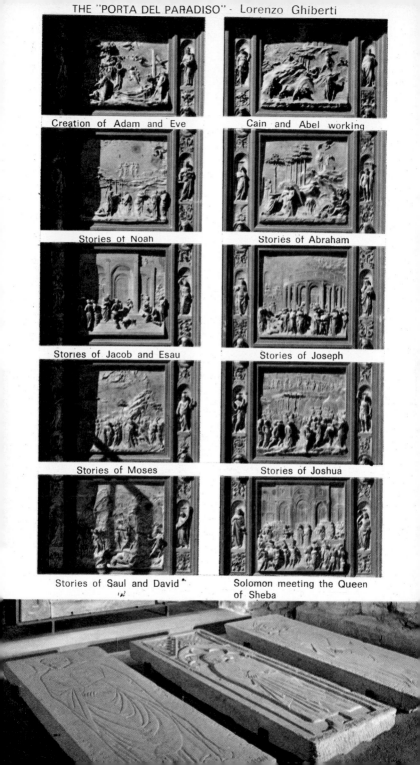

THE "PORTA DEL PARADISO" - Lorenzo Ghiberti

Creation of Adam and Eve

Cain and Abel working

Stories of Noah

Stories of Abraham

Stories of Jacob and Esau

Stories of Joseph

Stories of Moses

Stories of Joshua

Stories of Saul and David

Solomon meeting the Queen of Sheba

The Cathedral

CATHEDRAL OF SANTA MARIA DEL FIORE

The Cathedral of Florence is the third largest church in the world, exceeded only by St. Peter's in Rome and St. Paul's in London.

Arnolfo di Cambio was responsible for the original plan of the Cathedral and began to build it in 1296. After his death in 1301, the work was carried on by **Giotto,** who was also engaged in building the Campanile beside it. From 1337, the work was

CATHEDRAL: interior

continued by Francesco Talenti, who made some modifications to Arnolfo's original plan, especially with regard to the larger dimensions of the aisles, and the Cathedral was completed by Giovanni di Lapo Ghini in 1369. The cupola is the work of Filippo Brunelleschi, who, between 1420 and 1426, built it; it is a masterpiece both artistically and technically, since the artist had to solve the difficult problem of building it without a fixed framework; this he did by throwing the weight of the construction onto a smaller, inside cupola, and relying on the use of the so-called herring-bone stonework. The lantern at the top of the cupola is likewise the work of **Brunelleschi.**

It was only in 1887 that the façade was built by **Emilio De Fabris,** the one begun by Arnolfo di Cambio having been demolished in 1587.

Recently the foundations of the ancient church of *Santa Reparata* have been discovered under the building. The ancient perimetral structures of the church have come to light and interesting remains of monumental elements can be admired, such as the fine flooring, the columns, the mural paintings and tomb slabs. The crypt — very suggestive — on a whole is open for worship.

INTERIOR: This is in the form of a Latin cross (i.e. the longitudinal arm is longer than the transverse arm), and is divided into three aisles, separated by two rows of large, cruciform pillars, surmounted by pointed arches which give a slender elegance to the whole.

CATHEDRAL - Michelangelo: The « Pietà »

TRANSEPT AND APSE:

1) Octagonal choir with bas-reliefs by Bandinelli (1555); 2) Crucifixion (by Benedetto da Majano 1459-97); 3) Terracottas by Luca della Robbia (The Ascension - 1450); 4) Pietà by Michelangelo (1555): 1st Chapel.

This is one of the masterpieces of Michelangelo Buonarroti's late work. Although it was unfinished and the figure of Mary Magdalene, — the work of Tiberio Calcagni was added after his death — it appears in its full organic unity and beauty. The theme of the « Descent from the Cross » which Michelangelo had often studied and portrayed, is expressed here very dramatically, as can be seen from the continuous intertwining and contortions of the bodies which yet unite to form a single mass of great poetic intensity.

Filippo Brunelleschi: Cupola of the Cathedral

GIOTTO'S CAMPANILE

The Campanile is a very fine example of Florentine Gothic art and also bears testimony to **Giotto's** great artistic ability.

He began its construction in 1334 and continued with it until 1337, the year of his death, completing the first stage. The work was carried on by **Andrea Pisano** who built the second stage, but without the mullioned windows planned by his predecessor, thus departing from Giotto's original project. In 1348, Talenti reverted to the original idea, and brought it to completion, following it faithfully, except, perhaps, for the topmost part, where the Campanile terminates with a terrace affording a fine view, instead of with a point as planned.

The whole of the first stage is covered with two rows of panels, the work of various artists, including **Andrea Pisano, Alberto Arnoldi** and **Luca della Robbia**, completing a cycle planned by Giotto himself. The panels show liberal arts, trades, planets; virtues and sacraments.

LOGGIA DEL BIGALLO

This was built in the late Gothic style by **Alberto Arnoldi,** 1352-58, for the **Fraternity of the Misericordia,** which used to put abandoned children on view there.

In the arcades, very fine bas-reliefs by **Arnoldi, Nino Pisano** and others. In the interior, an interesting fresco of the Madonna della Misericordia.

MUSEUM « OPERA DEL DUOMO »

This museum is at no. 9 Piazza del Duomo, opposite the back of the Cathedral.

Here are preserved pieces coming from the Baptistery, the Cathedral and the Campanile, together with architectural remains from previous buildings on the site.

ROOM I: Here are the remains of the ancient baptismal font, removed from the Baptistery in 1577 (Dante was baptised in this), and the old altar

ROOM II: This contains fragments of the façade begun by Arnolfo di Cambio, which was left unfinished, and then demolished in 1587, and also the statues made for it:

St. John the Evangelist (by Donatello) which is said to have inspired Michelangelo; St. Luke (by Nanni Di Banco); Boniface VIII (school of Arnolfo di Cambio); Madonna and Child (by Arnolfo di Cambio); Madonna laid in the Tomb (by Arnolfo di Cambio); Nativity (by Arnolfo di Cambio).

ROOM III: Precious sacred objects and reliquaries are preserved here.
— We cross Room I to reach the upper floor.

ROOM IV: Also known as the « Room of the Choir Galleries », since it contains the two choirs by Luca della Robbia (1431-38) and Donatello (1433-39). The former illustrates the last of the Psalms of David; « Praise Him with the sound of the trumpet: praise Him with the loud-sounding cymbals »; and in truth the sound of the cymbals seems to burst forth from this creation, at once so classical and so full of joyous rhythm.
The latter shows a dance of cherubs whose intertwining movements display greater vitality than is to be seen in della Robbia's work: this is a distinguishing feature of Donatello's art, as compared with the lyrical sweetness of Luca della Robbia.
In the same room, other sculptures by Donatello are displayed, such as his Moses, Jeremiah and Habakkuk, also called « Zuccone ».

ROOM V: (adjoining Room IV), is also known as the « Room of the Panels », as it contains some of the panels carved for the Campanile by Andrea Pisano (probably to designs by Giotto), representing the cycle of « Man's progress towards civilization ».

ROOM VI: This is taken up by the **Silver Reredos,** a masterpiece of the Florentine goldsmiths' art of the 14th and 15th centuries. On it, scenes from the life of St. John the Baptist are depicted.
There are also 27 interesting pieces of embroidery, portraying events from his life, worked to the design of Pollaiolo, and a marquetry triptych with St. Zenobius and two saints, by Giuliano da Majano.

MUSEUM « FIRENZE COM'ERA »
(« BYGONE FLORENCE »)

From behind the Cathedral, by Via dell'Oriuolo and Via Portinari, we reach the ancient convent of the Oblate (lay-sisters), opposite the Hospital of Santa Maria Nuova. Here the Museum « Firenze com'era », is housed, in which there are engravings and drawings showing the evolution and development of Florence throughout the centuries.

Two panels of the Campanile: Creation of Adam and Eve ➤ (Andrea Pisano)

Choristers (Luca della Robba)   Abakkuk (Donatello)

ITINERARY II

FROM PIAZZA DEL DUOMO TO PIAZZA DELLA SIGNORIA
1) Piazza della Signoria - 2) Palazzo Vecchio - 3) Loggia della Signoria - 4) Palazzo degli Uffizi - 5) Uffizi Gallery

PIAZZA DELLA SIGNORIA

Following Via dei Calzaiuoli from the Piazza del Duomo, we reach the fine large **Piazza della Signoria**. For centuries, it has been the centre of the political life of Florence and the scene of its main historical events from the Middle Ages almost to the present time.

Every year, the Game of **Football in historical costume** is played in this square.

FOUNTAIN OF NEPTUNE

To the left of **Palazzo Vecchio** is the famous fountain of Neptune, by **Bartolomeo Ammannati** who worked on it from 1560 to 1575, together with **Giambologna.**

It consists of a series of austerely elegant bronze statues, representing marine divinities and satyrs, and culminates in the colossal marble statue of Neptune in the centre, an unsuccessful attempt on the part of Ammannati to imitate Michelangelo.

Because of this, the people of Florence have jokingly nicknamed it the « Biancone » (« the pasty one ») and still repeat an ironical epigram about its sculptor: **Ammannato Ammannato, che bel marmo hai rovinato.** « *Ammannato, Ammannato, what a beatiful marble you have spoiled* ».

PALAZZO VECCHIO
(Old Palace)

The Palazzo Vecchio, also known as « Palazzo della Signoria » or « Palazzo del Popolo » was built between 1298 and 1314; it is probably based on an unknown plan of Arnolfo di Cambio. The massive square building, covered with typical rustic ashlar, is lightened by the elegant mullioned windows and the splendid tower, erected on a previous one, known as the Tower dei Foraboschi.

The Palazzo Vecchio was the old residence of the Medici, the rulers of Florence, until Cosimo I moved the seat of the government to Palazzo Pitti, (1550).

The steps in front of the Palazzo are adorned by the following statues:

The « Marzocco », the symbolic lion of the Florentine Republic; the group by Donatello of **Judith and Holofernes** (1460); copy of Michelangelo's David and the group of **Hercules and Cacus** by **Baccio Bandinelli** (1536).

INTERIOR: the main door leads directly to the **first Courtyard,** restored in 1453 by Michelozzo in the Renaissance style, but later made heavy by stuccos of the 16th century. In the cen-

PALAZZO VECCHIO

tre stands a copy of Verrocchio's **« Winged Cupid with Dolphin »**. The original has been moved to the 2nd floor.

FIRST FLOOR: By way of the grand staircase, the work of Vasari (1560-63), we reach the

Salone dei Cinquecento (53 metrès long, 22 wide and 18 high): this is one of the most monumental halls in public palaces. Built by Cronaca (1495) for the meetings of the Grand Council of the Republic.

OLD PALACE - « Victory » (Michelangiolo)

Among the sculptures in the Hall, Michelangelo's « **Victory** » group (niche on S. side), intended for the tomb of Julius II, and the six statues of the « **Labours of Hercules** » by Vincenzo de Rossi are particularly interesting.

Study of Francesco I: A small door to the right of the Hall leads to this. It is a veritable jewel-case, exquisitely decorated by Vasari. More precisely, it served as a sort of strong-room for the Duke: « **Il Tesoretto** » (the Little Treasury).

Sala dei Duecento, now taken over by the Municipality. It was built in the latter half of the fifteenth century, by Benedetto and Giuliano da Majano. We return to the Salone of the Cinquecento and, through the door located in front of the Study of Francesco I, we pass to the:

Medieval Chambers, the walls of which are devoted to the

OLD PALACE - Room of the Five Hundred

OLD PALACE - Hercules and Diomedes (Vincenzo de Rossi)

most important members of the Medici family. The frescoes are by Vasari.

Room of Cosimo the Elder; in the frescoes on the vault are portrayed scenes from the life of Cosimo the Elder. Of particular interest are those in which he is seen surrounded by artists and famous personalities of his time.

Room of Lorenzo the Magnificent: like the others, this has frescoes portraying scenes from the life of the member of the Medici family to whom it is dedicated.

Room of Duke Cosimo I with interesting frescoes showing him with famous people of his time.

SECOND FLOOR: We return to the Salone dei Cinquecento and thence to the 2nd floor, where we see the:

Quartiere degli elementi, built by Battista del Tasso and decorated by Vasari with subjects representing the four elements (earth, air, fire and water). It consists of

The Terrace of Saturn, with a wonderful view; Hercules Room, with scenes from the Labours of Hercules, work of Doceno; Jupiter Room, with 16th century precious tapestries; Cybele and Opis Room, with 18th century Florentine tapestries; Ceres Room, with works of Vasari.

Apartments of Eleanor of Toledo or of the Priors, where the wife of Cosimo I lived.

Green Room, (with grotesque vaults) with an interesting « Madonna and Child » by Botticelli's school; Eleanor Chapel, painted in frescoes by Bronzino; Sabine Room, of Eleanor's maids of honour, containing portraits of the Medici princes; Esther, or Dining Room, with a 15th century marble wash-basin and precious Florentine tapestries; Penelope Room, with frescoes painted in the manner of Botticelli. From the window we can enjoy a wonderful view of the Square of the Signoria; Room of the « fair Gualdrada » (Eleanor of Toledo), so called by Cosimo I in honour of his wife's fidelity. He had frescoes painted on the walls with stories of the famous « fair Gualdrada », daughter of Bellincione Berti immortalised by Dante.

Chapel of the Signoria, decorated with frescoes by Rodolfo Ghirlandaio in 1514.

Audience Chamber: built by Benedetto da Majano (1475-81). The fine ceiling is by Giuliano da Majano.

Lily Chamber: likewise the work of Benedetto da Majano, who executed the ceiling also.

Chancellery: large room dedicated to Niccolò Machiavelli who lived here as Secretary of the Florentine Republic.

Medici Wardrobe Room: this is reached through the main door of the Chancellery. Here the Medici kept their treasures. There is an interesting globe by Ignazio Danti and on the cupboards, carved by Dionigi Nigretti, 53 coloured maps have been painted. Both the globe and maps are of great scientific interest as showing what was known of the world in the 16th century. We go down to the ancient mezzanine floor to the five rooms where is housed the:

LOESER COLLECTION: among the most important works here are paintings by Bronzino and Pietro Lorenzetti, and sculptures by Donatello, Michelangelo, Tino di Camaino and Giambologna. Finally we can ascend the TOWER from which there is a wonderful view.

LOGGIA DELLA SIGNORIA

To the right of Palazzo Vecchio stands the Loggia della Signoria or « of the Priors », built between 1376 and 1382 by Benci di Cione and Simone Talenti. The architecture is particularly interesting, as it shows the persistence of the Gothic style together with the beginning of the new Renaissance spirit. It also has some very fine sculptures, among which we would mention:

1) Perseus: bronze statue by Benvenuto Cellini, 1533 (left

Perseus   Rape of the Sabine Women

arch); 2) *Rape of the Sabine Women, by Giambologna, 1559
(right arch); 3) Hercules and the Centaur, by Giambologna;
4) Menelaus bearing Patroclus: copy of the Greek original of
the 4th century B.C.; 5) Rape of Polyxena, by Fedi (1886).*

There are 6 other female statues, representing Roman mat-
rons and wives of Roman emperors.

UFFIZI PALACE

This is Vasari's largest and finest work, built by him for Cosimo I between 1560 and 1570. Its main feature is two long porticos terminating in a wide archway facing the Arno. In the niches of the great pilasters which alternate with the pairs of columns, a series of statues was added in the 19th century, representing the most famous personalities of Tuscany, such as: Benvenuto Cellini, Galileo Galilei, Francesco Ferrucci, Giovanni delle Bande Nere, Pier Capponi, Farinata degli Uberti, Amerigo Vespucci, Boccaccio, Petrarca, Dante, Michelangelo, Leonardo, Leon Battista Alberti, Donatello, Giotto, Nicola Pisano, Orcagna, Cosimo the Elder, and Lorenzo the Magnificent.

UFFIZI GALLERY

This is the largest and most famous picture gallery in italy and one of the best-known in the world, housing the greatest treasures of Italian and foreign art. The main entrance is at the beginning of the left portico. The famous « Vasariano » corridor, crossing the « Ponte Vecchio », joins the Uffizi Gallery with Pitti Palace. (Palatine Gallery).

GROUND FLOOR

In the ENTRANCE HALL are busts and tapestries of members of the Medici family and of the House of Lorraine.

VESTIBULE: here are the remains of ancient columns from San Pietro Scheraggio (a Romanesque church consecrated in 1068) which had been built on the site now occupied by the Palazzo degli Uffizi. The Church, after careful restoration, has recently been reopened to the public.

By VASARI'S STAIRCASE with 126 stairs (or by the lift) we reach the

FIRST FLOOR

CABINET OF DRAWINGS AND ENGRAVINGS: The is one of the richest in the world, started by Cardinal Leopold de' Medici and later enlarged. It contains a vast collection of drawings of the best Italian and foreign artists. Exhibitions of graphic art are held from time to time in the 1st Room.

THIRD FLOOR

The gallery proper begins here.

LEFT GALLERY OR FIRST CORRIDOR: its vaults are decorated with grotesque paintings (by Butteri, Allori and others). On the walls are 16th century tapestries showing various subjects such as Hunting scenes, the Months of the Year, and Feasts of Henry III and Caterina de' Medici.

All along the corridor are sarcophagi, busts and statues from Roman times (for the most part copies of the originals).

ROOM I, called the « **Hermaphrodite Room** », after the statue of that name in the middle, which is a Roman copy of a Hellenistic original . Propped up against the walls are fragments of bas-reliefs, fronts of sarcophagi and busts, including one of Cicero.

ROOM II : works of the Tuscan School of the 13th and 14th centuries:

Loggia della Signoria ➤

Piazzale degli Uffizi

Crucifix and stories of the life of Christ (13th century); Stories of St. Cecilia: the work of an unknown pupil of Giotto, commonly called, from this picture the "Master of St. Cecilia"; Madonna with Child (13th century); Madonna Enthroned, with Angels: famous work by Cimabue, the great Tuscan painter who succeeded in overcoming the Byzantine influence and was probably Giotto's teacher; Madonna Enthroned: by Duccio di Buoninsegna, who, like Cimabue, was a protagonist of the new Florentine style of painting, imbuing his work with a lyricism from which the whole Sienese School would take its cue; Madonna Enthroned: work of Giotto (1310) painted for the Church of Ognissanti.

ROOM III: Sienese School of the 14th century.

Works by Ambrogio Lorenzetti:
The Presentation in the Temple (1342); Stories of St. Nicholas of Bari; San Procolo; St. Nicholas.
Works by Pietro Lorenzetti:
Saints; Madonna with Child and Angels (1341); Stories of the Blessed Humility.
Works by Simone Martini:
Annunciation (1333); a painting of exquisite elegance, both for the luminosity of its colours and the fluidity of its Gothic line, of which the artist was one of the most sensitive exponents.

ROOM IV: works of the Florentine 14th century, for the most part in the tracks of Giotto:
Madonna with Child and Angels (Taddeo Gaddi); The Descent from the Cross (Giottino); Madonna Enthroned with Child (Bernardo Daddi); St. Matthew and scenes from his life (Orcagna); The Crucifixion (Taddeo Gaddi).

ROOMS V AND VI: Florid or International Gothic XIV and early XV centuries:
The Thebaid; The Adoration of the Magi: 1423, by Gentile da Fabriano, full of rustic freshness and loving attention to the costumes of the time; Four Saints (Gentile da Fabriano); The Crowning of the Virgin, with stories of St. Benedict; 1413, by Lorenzo Monaco; The Adoration of the Magi (Lorenzo Monaco).

ROOM VII (approached through Room II).
This contains the works of the Early Florentine Renaissance (beginning of XV century):
Battle of San Romano, by Paolo Uccello: one of the three battle scenes painted by the artist - the other two are in the Louvre and the National Gallery at London respectively; Madonna with St. Anne and Angels (1424); by Masolino. We recognise also the hand of Masaccio in the group of the Madonna and Child which is distinguished from the rest by a greater sense of volume and perspective. Madonna Enthroned between Saints (Domenico Veneziano); Portrait of Frederick of Montefeltro and Battista Sforza: 1466, by Piero della Francesca; Triptych of St. Juvenal; 1422. This work was rediscovered at San Giovanni at Cascia near Florence in 1961.

ROOM VIII: Filippo Lippi and his pupils. Among the works of Filippo Lippi, a sensitive artist of great delicacy, we would mention:
Madonna with Child and Saints; The Crowning of the Virgin; Virgin adoring the Child.

Other outstanding paintings here are:

The Annunciation; Stories of St. Benedict (Baldovinetti); St. Vincent, St. James and St. Eustace (Antonio and Piero del Pollaiolo); The Crowning of the Virgin (by Fra Angelico).

ROOM IX: this room is devoted to Pollaiolo and Botticelli:

Series of Virtues (by Antonio and Piero del Pollaiolo); Portrait of Galeazzo Sforza (Pollaiolo).

Botticelli is an artist of exquisite delicacy and fine sensitivity, expressing his personality in a melancholy, musical style, with a sweet harmony of line; in his paintings, the classical myths of Venus, Zephyr and Flora, come to life again, inspired by the poetry of Ovid and Poliziano. Among his works, which are displayed in various rooms, we would mention:

The Fortress; Holofernes; The Return of Judith; Portrait of an unknown man; Virgin with Child (3 paintings).

ROOM X: This is devoted to Botticelli's masterpieces:

Spring (1476-78) executed for Lorenzo de' Medici; Tondo of the Magnificat (1484); The Birth of Venus (1482), likewise for Lorenzo de' Medici; The Adoration of the Magi (1474).

ROOM XI: Works by Botticelli and Filippo Lippi.
Allegory of Calumny: 1498 by Botticelli.

This was painted after the violent death of Savonarola, whose preaching of asceticism had greatly influenced him.

ROOM XII: This is devoted to Flemish artists working in Italy:
3 portraits (by Hans Memling); Madonna (Hans Memling); Christ borne to the Sepulchre (Rogier van der Weyden).

ROOM XIII: Florentine painting of the second half of the 15th century, influenced by Botticelli and Ghirlandaio:
Portrait (by Filippino Lippi); Self-portrait (by Filippino Lippi); Allegory (by Filippino Lippi); Annunciation (by Botticelli).

ROOM XIV: This contains paintings by Van der Goes, a Flemish artist, and by Tuscan painters of the 15th century who were influenced by him:
The Portinari Triptych; in the centre, the Adoration of the Shepherds, at the sides, the figures of Saints and of the patrons: we note here a care of detail and that vivid sense of colour and nature which is characteristic of Flemish art; Triptych of the Resurrection (by Nicolas Froment); Virgin on the Throne (by Ghirlandaio); Virgin with Child, Angels and Saints (Ghirlandaio); The Adoration of the Magi (by Lorenzo di Credi); Madonna with Child and Saints (Filippino Lippi).

ROOM XV: This is devoted to the foremost Umbrian painters (Signorelli, Perugino and others), to the Tuscan painters of the second half of the fifteenth century (Verrocchio) and to Leonardo:
The Annunciation (by Lorenzo di Credi); The Holy Family (Luca Signorelli); Madonna with Child and two Saints (Perugino); The Crucifixion (Perugino); The Holy Trinity (Perugino); Madonna and Angels (Piero di Cosimo); The Baptism of Christ (Verrocchio). This painting is of particular interest because in it we see for first time the hand of Leonardo, easily recognisable in the gentle expression and the soft flow of the draperies of the Angel on the left, and in the technique of colour shading in the landscape. The Adoration of the Magi (1481), by Leonardo.

Although it is unfinished, it has all the characteristics of the supreme artist: from the compact organisation of the whole, enveloped in a dim half-light, the figures of the Virgin with the Child and the adoring Shepherds suddenly emerge.

ROOM XVI: also called the **Map Room:**

The Annunciation (1475) a work of the youthful Leonardo, in which, in spite of the wholly traditional concept of the subject, we note already some of the artist's characteristic features, such as the soft shading of the distant landscape and a careful and loving observation of nature, derived from his study of natural science; Portrait (Lorenzo di Credi).

ROOM XVII: (after crossing Room XV and going back along the corridor, we reach this room by way of Room XVIII):

The Annunciation (Luca Signorelli); The Adoration of the Magi (Luca Signorelli); The Nativity (Luca Signorelli); Stories of the Passion (Luca Signorelli); Allegories of fruitfulness (Luca Signorelli); The Baptist (Melozzo da Forli); St. Benedict (Melozzo da Forli).

ROOM XVIII; also called « **The Tribune** ». This room is the work of Buontalenti (1588) and was specially built to house the masterpieces of the Medici collection.

Notable among the sculptures are the following:

UFFIZI GALLERY - « Annunciation » (Botticelli)

The Medici Venus (in the centre of the room), a famous copy of a Greek original; The Knife grinder; The Wrestlers (3rd century B.C.); The Dancing Faun; Satyr; Apollo.

and among the paintings:

Eleanor di Toledo; Don Garcia de' Medici; Bartolomeo Panciatichi: all portraits by Bronzino; Maria Salviati (portrait by Pontormo); Lorenzo the Magnificent (portrait by Vasari).

ROOM XIX: works by Perugino and his school:

2 portraits of Vallombrosian monks; Portrait of a Young Man; The Descent from the Cross; Francesco delle Opere.

In addition there are paintings by Francesco Francia and Lorenzo Costa.

ROOM XX: Paintings by Andrea Mantegna and Dürer, a German artist who came under his influence during his stay in Italy:

Triptych of the Adoration of the Magi, by Andrea Mantegna; The Ascension and the Circumcision, by Andrea Mantegna; Portrait of the artist's father (1490); Madonna and Child; Adam and Eve, by Duerer; The Road to Calvary; Adam and Eve; portrait of Luther and his wife, by Cranach; St. Dominic (Cosmé Tura).

ROOM XXI: Fifteenth Century Venetian School (Giovanni Bellini and Giorgione).
Among the works, we would mention:

Pietà; Portrait of a man; Allegory of Purgatory; The Judgement of Solomon (by Giorgione); Moses before Pharoah (by Giorgione); St. James and St. Philip (Carpaccio); Madonna (Cima da Conegliano).

ROOM XXII: devoted to the Flemish and German painters of the 16th century; among them, Hans Holbein, painter of famous portraits, and Gerard David, whose Adoration of the Magi we single out for special mention.

ROOM XXIII: devoted to Antonio Allegri (1489-1534), called « Correggio » after his native town. Of his works, we would mention:

Repose in Egypt (1516); Madonna and Child.

ROOM XXIV: this contains a series of miniatures by Italian and foreign artists, from the 15th to the 18th century.

SECOND CORRIDOR: this joins the two wings of the Uffizi Gallery. It contains classical Greek and Roman sculptures, including:

Boy extracting a Thorn from his foot (also called the « Spinario »), of the 5th century B. C.; Venus in her Bath; A circular altar showing the Sacrifice of Iphigenia.

RIGHT-HAND GALLERY or THIRD CORRIDOR: This contains sculptures of the 3rd and 4th centuries B.C., among them various portraits of Roman personalities, the two statues of Marsyas (copies of Hellenistic originals) and the marble group by Baccio Bandinelli (16th century), a copy of the famous Greek Laocoon. On the walls are three series of tapestries: Stories of the Passion (of Florentine manufacture), and Stories of Jacob and of Battles (manufactured in Brussels).

ROOM XXVI: Raphael and Michelangelo:

Madonna with Goldfinch (1506): this painting by Raphael reminds us of the pyramidal composition and sweetness of expression which are characteristic of Leonardo's style; Portrait of Pope Leo X; Portrait of Pope Julius II.

Among the works of Michelangelo, an artist of more dramatic and baffling spirit, in contrast with Raphael's gentle and lyrical tones, are the following:

UFFIZI GALLERY - Madonna with Goldfinch (Raffaello)

UFFIZI GALLERY - Holy Family (Michelangiolo)

The Doni Tondo (1504-1505), showing the Holy Family: this work is a good example of Michelangelo's particular conception of plastic values — these are expressed in movement and in spiral lines, in a continuous contortion of the bodies and in the powerful placement of the figures in space.

In this room, we also find works of minor artists who felt the influence of these two great masters, achieving, however, only a superficial and mannered style.

ROOM XXVI: this contains the works of Andrea del Sarto (the « fautless painter ») and some mannerists.
Portrait; Figures and Stories of Saints; The Madonna of the Harpies, renowned for its balanced composition and for the softly suffused chiaroscuro.

Among other works are:
Portrait of a young Woman (Rosso Fiorentino); Moses defending the Daughters of Jethro (Rosso Fiorentino); Portrait of St. Anthony (Pontormo).

ROOM XXVII: contains works by Pontormo, the most interesting and original of the Tuscan mannerists.
Leda with Swan; The Supper at Emmaus; Madonna and Child with the Infant St. John; Madonna with Child and Saints.

In this room, works by other artists such as Rosso Fiorentino and Beccafumi are also displayed.

ROOM XXVIII: devoted to Titan, the Venetian painter who developed more colourfully the tonal technique of Bellini and Giorgione:
Portrait of Caterina Cornaro (copy of the original); Flora.
Venus with lap-dog (1538), also known as the « Venus of Urbino », a painting remarkable for its delicacy and the light and shade of the beautiful nude and for the warm luminosity which pervades all the surroundings; Portrait of a Knight of Malta.

We would mention the following work of Palma il Vecchio who followed in Titian's steps: *Judith.*

ROOM XXIX: devoted to the works of Parmigianino, Francesco Mazzola (1505-1540) and to the Emilian School of the 16th century:

ROOM XXX: completes Room XXIX:
The Madonna of San Zaccaria, by Parmigianino; Repose in Egypt (Dono Doni).

ROOM XXXI: contains the largest paintings of Dono Doni, a Venetian artist whose chief characteristics are vivid colouring and luminosity:

ROOM XXXII, also devoted to the work of Venetian artists of the 16th century:

ROOM XXXIII: This is a corridor in which are displayed the works of Italian and foreign artists of the late 16th century; among these, we would mention Vasari, Allori, Bronzino, Clouet, Morales and Mor.

ROOM XXXIV: works by Veronese, one of the foremost Venetian artists. He is essentially a painter of costume, and portrayed the sumptuous Venetian society of his time, enriching his paintings with a vivid sense of colour and movement, combined with a marked preciousness, portending the birth of the Baroque style:

ROOM XXXV: devoted to Tintoretto. With this artist, the tonalism which had been the dominant feature of Venetian painting, takes on a vivid luminosity.

ROOM XXXVI (The works displayed in Rooms 36,37, 38, 39 and 40 have been temporarily removed to other rooms): dedoted to Caravaggio and the painters of the Carracci family.

ROOM XXXVII

2 portraits by Rembrandt; Portrait of an Old Man (Rembrandt); works by Jan Lys, a Flemish painter; works by Domenico Fedi and Bernardo Strozzi.

ROOM XXXVIII: Italian School of the 18th century.

In this room there are fragments of a ceiling painted by G. Battista Tiepolo, a Venetian painter, who carried the luminous tonality of Venetian painting to its extreme limits, creating an air perspective in which air and light become the very essence of things.

ROOM XXXIX: Venetian painting of the 18th century. The outstanding artists of the period are Canaletto and Guardi who depicted the Venice of their day in a delicate and dreamy atmosphere.

UFFIZI GALLERY - Venus with lap-dog (or Venus of Urbino) Tiziano

ROOM XL: this contains works by Crespi, an artist concerned with everyday life in its humblest aspects.

ROOM XLI: devoted to Rubens, a painter of particular passion and sensitivity, who commemorated official events.

ROOM XLII: or **Niobe Room.**

sculptured group of Niobe and her children. Roman copies of Greek originals of the 3rd — 2nd century B.C. Works of French painters of the 18th century are temporarily displayed here.

Michelangelo Merisi, known as **Caravaggio,** revolutionised the whole of 16th century Italian painting, not only by concentrating on powerful light effects which reveal the most dramatic and intimate moments of a person or an event, but also by restoring to art a keen sense of reality, sometimes shown in its crudest but most meaningful aspects.

The Young Bacchus: an early work, which already foretells the artist's future development, although classical influences can still be observed.

UFFIZI GALLERY - Young Bacchus (Caravaggio)

CHURCH OF SANTA CROCE

ITINERARY III

1) Piazza di Santa Croce - 2) Basilica di Santa Croce - 3) Cloisters of Santa Croce - 4) Pazzi Chapel - 5) Santa Croce Museum - 6) Michelangelo's House - 7) Horne Museum - 8) Bardini Museum

PIAZZA DI SANTA CROCE
(Santa Croce Square)

The Piazza, which is dominated by the **Church of Santa Croce,** is surrounded on the other sides by ancient Florentine Palaces, including (on the left) **Palazzo Serristori** (1470) built by Baccio d'Agnolo and **Palazzo d'Antella** (1619). Immediately to the right of Piazza Santa Croce, at no. 5 Via Giuseppe Verdi, stands the Verdi Theatre.

BASILICA OF SANTA CROCE

« But most blessed thou, who dost preserve the glories of Italy, gathered in a temple ». Thus Foscolo addressed Florence in his « Sepolcri », since it preserves in the Church of Santa Croce the tombs and monuments of the greatest men in the history and literature of Italy, and where he himself is buried.

CHURCH OF SANTA CROCE - Interior

Built to a plan probably by Arnolfo di Cambio, about 1294-95 for the Franciscan Order of the Minorites, to replace a small, ancient church, it underwent various changes, above all in the façade, which is the work of Nicola Matas (1853-63) who tried to imitate and restore the Tuscan Gothic style.

THE INTERIOR is built to a « T » shape plan (Egyptian cross) and is divided into three aisles. The arches are of particular interest:
pointed, after the Gothic style of the period, and are, as it were, checked in their upward surge and brought back to a classical restraint by a horizontal gallery above the arches and by the trussed roof (a regular feature of Franciscan churches).

RIGHT AISLE: here we can admire the tombs and monuments of illustrious men and other works of great interest.
1st altar: « The Crucifixion » (by Santi di Tito).
1st pilaster: « Madonna Nursing » (by Antonio Rossellino).
Opposite: Tomb of Michelangelo, sculpted by Vasari about 1570.
2nd altar: « The Road to Calvary » (by Vasari).

Between 2nd and 3rd altar: Cenotaph of Dante, the work of Stefano Ricci (1829). The poet's tomb is at Ravenna, where he died in exile.

Between the 3rd and 4th altar: Monument to Vittorio Alfieri, by Canova (1810), which in its essential lines, is an example of the neo-classical style of this sculptor.

Pilaster opposite (3rd): pulpit by Benedetto da Majano (1475) depicting the life of St. Francis.

Between the 4th and 5th altar: monument to Niccolò Machiavelli by Innocenzo Spinazzi (1787).

40

5th altar: fresco painting of « Christ in the Garden » by Andrea del Minga. The rear part of the picture is more interesting: it shows « The Triumph of Death » by Orcagna (1348), painted with an impressive sense of realism. This picture has been placed in the Santa Croce Museum.

Further on: « St. John the Baptist » and « St. Francis », by Domenico Veneziano.

Tabernacle of statuary stone and gold by Donatello (1430), showing the Annunciation, one of the masterpieces of the great artist.

Tomb of Leonardo Bruni (1444) by Rossellino. This is of particular importance as being the prototype of Florentine tombs from 15th century on.

Monument to Gioacchino Rossini (by Cassioni).

6th Altar: on the left, is the tomb of Ugo Foscolo, the great poet who had sung the praises of the Basilica of Santa Croce for having gathered to itself such a company of illustrious men.

SANTA CROCE - Tomb of Michelangiolo (G. Vasari)

SANTA CROCE - Pulpit by Benedetto da Majano

RIGHT ARM OF THE CROSS:

Castellani Chapel or Chapel of the Holy Sacrament: this preserves an important cycle of frescoes:

Right: frescoes by Agnolo Gaddi and his son Taddeo (14th century) with stories of St. Nicholas of Bari and of the Baptist.
Left: Stories of St. John the Evangelist and St. Anthony the Abbot (Agnolo Gaddi and Taddeo Gaddi).

Baroncelli Chapel: decorated by Taddeo Gaddi, a pupil of Giotto, with scenes from the life of the Virgin.

On the back wall is « The Madonna with the Girdle » by Sebastiano Bainardi (of Ghirlandaio's workshop) and « The Crowning of the Virgin », signed by Giotto, but more probably to be attributed to his pupil, Taddeo Gaddi.

Sacristy: the doorway after the Baroncelli Chapel leads to the sacristy corridor with barrel vaults and elegant three mullioned windows, the work of Michelozzo. In the Sacristy there are frescoes by Antonio and Pietro Gerini, depicting stories of the Passion. In the back wall of the Sacristy is the

SANTA CROCE - Tabernacle by Donatello

Rinuccini Chapel with frescoes of stories from the life of Mary Magdalene and the Virgin Mary, by Giovanni da Milano and his assistants.

Returning to the church, we see in the transept eleven Chapels which have been altered in later times.

1) **Velluti Chapel:** contains fresco paintings by pupils of Cavallini and Cimabue (end of 13th century) with stories of St. Michael the Archangel.

2) **Calderini, later Riccardi, Chapel:** the original frescoes by Taddeo Gaddi were covered over and it was later decorated by Gherardo Silvani and Giovanni da San Giovanni.

SANTA CROCE - Burial of St. Francis - Detail (Giotto)

3) **Giugni, later Bonaparte, Chapel:** to the left stands the tomb of Carlotta Bonaparte; to the right, that of Giulia Bonaparte Clary.

4) **Peruzzi Chapel:** contains a cycle of frescoes by Giotto (1320) with stories of St. John the Evangelist. These were whitewashed over, in 1714, and brought to light again in 1841; they were badly restored by Marini in 1863. Attempts are now being made to bring them back to their original condition.

Right wall: Vision on the Island of Patmos:

The Saint raises Druisiana from the dead. Stories of St. John the Baptist.

Left wall: The Angel's annunciation to Zaccharias: Birth of the Baptist. Herod's Feast.

Above the Altar: « St. Francis and Stories of his Life » (an interesting work by an unknown artist of the 13th century).

5) **Bardi Chapel:** this too was entirely decorated by Giotto in 1317 and is one of his most important works. As in the Church of St. Francis at Assisi, stories from the life of St. Francis are depicted here, but with greater artistic maturity and better combination of mass and light.

Above the Altar; a painting on wood with stories of St. Francis (Berlinghieri, 13th century).

6) **Maggiore or degli Alberti Chapel:** with frescoes by Agnolo Gaddi, depicting the Legend of the Holy Cross, a cycle of stories in which Giotto's influence is superimposed upon the prevailing Gothic trend.

Above the Altar: polyptych with Madonna and Saints. The central part is the work of Niccolò di Pietro Gerini. The crucifix over the altar is by one of Giotto's pupils.

7) **Tosinghi, formerly Sloane Chapel,** originally decorated with frescoes by Giotto and his pupils, and completely altered at the beginning of the 19th century.

Above the Altar: polyptych with Madonna and Saints, by Giovanni del Biondo.

8) **Capponi or St. Anne's Chapel:** dedicated to Italian mothers The marble Pietà is the work of Libero Andreotti (1926).

9) **Ricasoli Chapel, or Chapel of St. Anthony of Padua:** this was completely restored in the 19th century. On the walls, paintings by Sabatelli and his sons.

10) **Pulci, later Bardi di Libertà, Chapel:** contains frescoes by Bernardo Daddi, showing the Martyrdom of St. Lawrence on the right, and the Martyrdom of St. Stephen on the left (first half of 14th century). In addition to the close composition copied directly from Giotto, they show a soft, clear sense of colour, which envelopes the figures in a poetic atmosphere of unreality.

Above the Altar: altar-piece portraying the Madonna and Saints, the work of Giovanni della Robbia.

11) **Bardi di Vernio Chapel:** here is the fine cycle of frescoes with stories of St. Sylvester, by Maso di Banco (1340), perhaps the best of Giotto's pupils. The following chapels are situated in the left arm of the cross.

LEFT ARM OF THE CROSS:

12) **Niccolini Chapel:** the vault is decorated by Volterrano (17th century). On the walls: tombs of the Niccolini family.

13) **Bardi Chapel:** this contains Donatello's famous crucifix, which Brunelleschi criticised as being too realistic.

14) **Salviati Chapel:** the tomb of Princess Sofia Zamoyski Czartryski, by Lorenzo Bartolini (19th century). On the left: Monument to Luigi Cherubini.

SANTA CROCE - Crucifix of Cimabue

LEFT AISLE: Going towards the exit of the Church, we see:
Monument to the engraver, Raffaello Morghen.

6th Altar: tomb of Carlo Marsuppini, a fine monument by Desiderio da Settignano who followed Rossellino's design for the tomb of Leonardo Bruni (right aisle).

Between the 5th and 6th altar: Monument to Vittorio Fossombroni (Bartolini).

5th Altar: « The Ascension », by Stradano (1569); « Pietà » (Bronzino).
In the floor, a tombstone dedicated to Lorenzo Ghiberti.
4th Altar: « The Doubting Thomas », by Vasari.

Monument to Galileo, by G. C. Foggini.

In the floor of the centre aisle of the Church, there are altogether 276 tombstones.

SANTA CROCE - Pazzi Chapel

CLOISTERS OF SANTA CROCE

To the right of the façade of the Basilica is the entrance to the beautiful Cloisters of Santa Croce. A slender and lofty arcade on the left, and a double loggia on the right, both of the 14th century, meet at the end in the lovely Pazzi Chapel, thus creating a silent and romantic setting, harmonious in all its parts.

SANTA CROCE MUSEUM

At the beginning of the 1st cloister, on the right, is the entrance to the Santa Croce Museum. It is housed in what was originally the Refectory of the Church, in one large room, which was unfortunately damaged, together with the works of art there displayed, by the flood of November 4th, 1966.

On the end wall fresco paintings by Taddeo Gaddi, recently restored, depicting (above) **« The Tree of the Cross »** and (below) **« The Last Supper »**, and others.

On the other walls are paintings formerly hung in the Church of Santa Croce, among them (on the left wall) « St. Francis » and « St. John the Baptist » by Domenico Veneziano and fragments of « The Triumph of Death » by Orcagna.

Among the sculptures is a very fine bronze statue of St. Louis of Toulouse by Donatello. After restoration, the famous **Crucifix of Cimabue,** which was badly damaged in the recent flood, will be put back in the Museum. It is a deeply felt, poetic composition, in which the intense drama expressed in the curve of Christ's suffering body is calmed and mitigated by the soft light and shade of the flesh and draperies.

47

PAZZI CHAPEL

This is one of the first examples of pure Renaissance spirit, in the restrained dignity of form, and the balance and classical harmony which dominate the whole building.

It is one of Brunelleschi's most important creations; he began work on it in 1430, continuing until 1446, when it was interrupted by his death. Indeed, the upper part of the façade has remained unfinished, where the architect had intended a dome like that of the Pantheon.

On leaving the Pazzi Chapel, we follow the arcade on the left. At the end of it, the second, beautiful **Cloister** opens up, likewise designed by Brunelleschi.

In Piazza dei Cavalleggeri, on the Lungarno, not far from Piazza di Santa Croce, stands the **National Library,** one of the most famous in Italy.

MICHELANGELO'S HOUSE

From Piazza Santa Croce, we follow Via de' Pepi and then Via Ghibellina where at No. 70 is the house of Michelangelo Buonarroti. It can also be reached by way of Via Pinzochere, likewise starting from the left side of Santa Croce, which brings one directly opposite Michelangelo's house.

Michelangelo Buonarroti was born at Caprese in 1475, and he started work as a sculptor in the Medici garden, under the guidance of Master Bertoldo, a pupil of Donatello. Michelangelo bought this house for his nephews who later decorated it with stories of the Buonarroti family.

In 1859, it was turned into a Museum to house the artist's early works.

Ground Floor: here is the Buonarroti Collection:

1st Floor: *On the right, as we enter, we find in the* 1st Room: *the Crucifix, an early work by Michelangelo, which is now with certainty attributed to him.* 2nd Room: *« River God », another of the artist's juvenile works.* 3rd Room: *Paintings of Michelangelo's school.* 4th Room: *« Madonna della Scala », a copy by Giambologna of the original displayed in another room.*

On the left as we enter, we find:
The Battle of the Centaurs. « Madonna della Scala ».

These are all youthful works, showing not only the classicistic influence of Donatello's latest experience of the « stiacciato » (Madonna della Scala), but also the power of expression and decisive line which are features of the artist's maturity.

In the next room are displayed drawings by Michelangelo as well as copies of projects and sketches of works carried out later.

The other rooms were the private apartments of the Buonarroti family.

HORNE MUSEUM

We go from Piazza Santa Croce along Via de Benci to reach the « Casa Horne », at no. 6, probably built by Giuliano da Sangallo. Here we find the HORNE MUSEUM which houses the valuable collection of works of art donated by the Englishman, Herbert Percy Horne, in 1916.

The following works are of particular interest:

Stories of St. Julian; Crucifix and Saints; Book of Drawings (Tiepolo); An old copy of Leonardo's « Battle of Anghiari ».

We would also mention works by:
Benozzo Gozzoli, Simone Martini, Beccafumi, Giambologna, Michelozzo and Luca della Robbia.

BARDINI MUSEUM

Continuing from Via de' Benci, we cross the Ponte delle Grazie, one of the oldest and soundest bridges of Florence, which was destroyed during the last war and faithfully rebuilt a few years ago. We now come to Piazza de' Mozzi where, on the left, we find the **Bardini Museum.**

The Bardini Palazzo, built in the 19th century, and donated by the antiquarian Bardini in 1923, is now a Museum with a collection of decorative sculpture, furniture, paintings, ceramics and arms from many sources.

MICHELANGELO'S HOUSE - The Battle of the Centaurs

ITINERARY IV

1) Dante's House - 2) Church of the Badia Fiorentina - 3) Palazzo of the Podestà or Bargello - 4) National or Bargello Museum - 5) Synagogue or Jewish Temple.

DANTE'S HOUSE

By way of Via Dante Alighieri, on the right of Via del Proconsolo, we find what is generally held to be the house of the greatest poet of Italian literature (1265-1321). The entrance is from Via Santa Margherita, and inside the palace are displayed in glass cases documents concerning Dante and the Alighieri family.

CHURCH OF THE BADIA FIORENTINA

Returning to Via del Proconsolo, we find the Benedictine Church founded on the orders of Willa, mother of Count Hugo of Tuscany, in 978. It was later enlarged (1285) and completely altered between 1625 and 1627 by Matteo Segaloni.

The rich doorway by Benedetto da Rovezzano (1475) is interesting. Above it we note the « Madonna and Child » by Buglioni; the very slender hexagonal campanile with four orders of mullioned windows, culminating in a sharp point, is also worthy of notice.

From the Sacristy, to the right of the apse, we pass to the **Small Cloister of the Orange Trees** with a series of fifteenth century fresco paintings depicting the Life of St. Benedict (on the 1st and 2nd storeys).

PALAZZO OF THE PODESTA' OR BARGELLO

The Palazzo del Podestà is at no. 4 Piazza San Firenze, a typical Florentine square of the fourteenth century. Built in 1225, it became the residence of the Chief Magistrate, then of the Podestà (or Mayor of Florence) and subsequently, in 1574, of the Chief of the Civil Police, also called « Bargello », hence the name of the Palace.

Since 1865 it has been the seat of the **National Museum of the Bargello.**

NATIONAL MUSEUM OF THE BARGELLO

This contains the most representative collection of Italian sculpture and decorative art. On entering, we immediately come to the
1st or ARMS ROOM: This was badly damaged in the flood of November 4, 1966, but has now been almost completely restored.

On the walls of the room and in the courtyard, interesting photographs are displayed, showing the condition of the exhibits the day after the inundation and the successive stages of restoration. On the walls are also a few remains of frescoes by 15th century painters.

NATIONAL MUSEUM OF THE BARGELLO

Most of the arms in this collection are of the 16th and 17th century, and the rich collection of Ressmann and Carrand has been added to them.

2nd or TOWER ROOM: Access to this is through the door to the left of the Arms Room. Some of the works previously displayed in the 4th Room have been placed here temporarily.

However, it will be put in order again, when it will contain arms, armour and flags of the 17th century.

In the centre, there stands at present:

Bacchus: *This is one of the earliest of Michelangelo's statues, and was commissioned from him by the Florentine banker Jacopo Gelli in 1496.*

The wine-god, although in a posture clearly deriving from classical models, is pervaded by a sense of grief and melancholy, which manifests itself in the weary curve of the body, the drooping head and the fixed and absent gaze of drunken eyes.

Leda with Swan: *a copy by Bartolomeo Ammannati of a similar group by Michelangelo;* Brutus: *a fine bust by Michelangelo (1540); Various copies of other works by Michelangelo.*

The COURTYARD is the finest and most picturesque part of the palace. It is surrounded on three sides by an arcade, while on the fourth there is a staircase, by Neri di Fioravanti, leading to the Balcony.

In the centre of the courtyard stands the cistern which served as a platform for viewing executions. Under the arcade there is a fine collection of sculptures.

ROOM OF 14th CENTURY SCULPTURES: Passing through the door at the back, opposite the door leading to the courtyard, we come to the 3rd room with sculptures of the 14th and 15th centuries by Tuscan artists.

Madonna and Child (Tino da Camaino); Stand for holy water stoup (Nicola Pisano).

1st FLOOR: We return to the courtyard and go up to the 1st floor. Along the balcony or loggia are sculptures and statues in bronze by Giambologna: Mercury, A Turkey, An Eagle, A Satyr 2 cherubs.

ROOM V or CHAMBER OF THE COUNCIL GENERAL: This is devoted to Donatello and other 15th century sculptors.

The Crucifixion, a bas-relief made with the « stiacciato » technique, testimony to Donatello's dramatic power; David, a bronze statue (1430); this depicts the figure of Renaissance man, who stands, serene and confident, at the centre of the world. The plastic values and harmony of form recall classical Greek sculpture; Tondo of the Madonna and Child by Michelangelo; St. John the Baptist; Marble statue of David; Marzocco; Athys, a bronze statuette distinguished by its brio, freshness and liveliness.

In this room there are also works by: Desiderio da Settignano « Madonna with Child », marble bas-relief which follows Donatello's « stiacciato » technique, with exquisitely delicate results.

Michelozzo: *2 « Madonna with Child ».*

Luca della Robbia: *« Madonna with Child »; « St. Peter freed from Prison »; « St. Peter Crucifield »; « Bust of a Woman ».*

6th or TOWER ROOM: This contains tapestries, fabrics and carpets from the Carrand Collection.

7th or PODESTA' ROOM: In this room, the Duke of Athens used to administer justice. It now contains jewellery and enamels from the 13th to the 16th century.

PODESTA' CHAPEL: Here prisoners condemned to death used to pray on their last day.

9th or JEWELLERY ROOM: containing sacred objects of great value.

10th or MAJOLICA ROOM: here majolica from Florence, Siena, Faenza, Urbino and Deruta is displayed (15th and 16th

BARGELLO - Bacchus (Michelangiolo)

century). We return to the Room of the Ivories and from there proceed to the

2nd FLOOR

11th ROOM: this is devoted to Benvenuto Cellini and Giovanni della Robbia. Amongst the works of Cellini, a Florentine sculptor, but above all goldsmith, we would mention:

Portrait of the Grand Duke Francis I; Perseus freeing Andromeda; Greyhound; Wax model of the Perseus in the Loggia of the Signoria, artistically preferable to the latter for the softer

BARGELLO - St. George - St. John the Baptist (Donatello)

modelling of the lines and for a greater overall freshness; Large bust of Cosimo I; Narcissus.

On the walls are enamelled terracottas by Giovanni della Robbia.

12th ROOM: this contains terracottas by Andrea della Robbia, nephew of Luca and father of Giovanni.

Bust of a Boy; Madonna with the Pillow.

13th ROOM: devoted to Verrocchio and Pollaiolo. Andrea del Verrocchio, the teacher of Leonardo and influenced by his pupil, was one of the greatest representatives of the second half of the 15th century.

*Bronze statue of David; Resurrection; Woman with Bouquet
(1470-75)* a serenely harmonious picture, in which, undoubtedly
under the influence of his famous pupil, Leonardo, he achieves
the soft shading characteristic of his famous pupil.

Pollaiolo is likewise one of the greatest representatives of
the later 15th century.
*A bronze group of Hercules and Antaeus; Young Warrior; Bust
of an Unknown Man.*
The room also contains works by other artists, viz: Mino da
Fiesole (portrait of Rinaldo della Luna); Antonio Rossellino (Madonna with Child); Benedetto da Maiano (portrait of Pietro Mel-
lini); Laurana (portrait of Battista Sforza) and others.

14th ROOM or ROOM WITH FIREPLACE: the famous stone
fireplace, from which the room gets its name, is the work of
Benedetto da Rovezzano. We reach it after returning to Room
12. The following works by Jacopo Sansovino are of particular
interest:

Madonna and Child; Bacchus with a Faun; Christ in Glory.
There are also sculptures by Vittoria and by Lorenzo Bernini
(1598-1680):
Costanza Buonarelli, one of Bernini's early works, modelled
when he was « passionately in love with her ».

15th ROOM or ROOM OF THE BRONZES: (reached through
Room XI). This room derives its name from the small bronzes
by various Renaissance and post-Renaissance artists displayed
there. Special mention should be made of Bernini's magnificent
bust of Costanza Buonarelli.

16th or TOWER ROOM: containing tapestries, brocades and
other fabrics manufactured in various towns.

BARGELLO - The Courtyard

17th ROOM or ROOM OF THE WAXES or OF THE PLAGUE: this derives its name from the representation of the plague in polychrome wax. The « Decomposition of the Corpses » is particularly realistic.

ROOM OF THE MEDAL COLLECTIONS: this room is generally not open to the public. It contains the most complete collection of Italian medals of every period. Among the finest and most important, those by Pisanello, Matteo de' Pasti and Benvenuto Cellini should be noted.

SYNAGOGUE

Turning from Via del Proconsolo into Via Pietrapiana, we reach Piazza Sant'Ambrogio where stands the ancient little church of **St. Ambrose,** one of the oldest sacred buildings in Florence, restored in the 13th century.

By Via dei Pilastri and Via Farini (on the left) we come to the Synagogue. It is an original building, whose forms and motifs show an Eastern inflence: its polychrome decoration is most picturesque. It is the work of the architects Falcini, Micheli and Treves (19th century).

SYNAGOGUE

ITINERARY V

1) Church of Orsanmichele - 2) Palace of the Wool Guild - 3) Loggia of the Mercato Nuovo - 4) Palace Davanzati and the Museum of the Florentine House - 5) Parte Guelfa Palace - 6) Church of the Holy Apostles - 7) Holy Trinity Church - 8) Holy Trinity Bridge - 9) Spini-Ferroni Palace - 10) Strozzi Palace - 11) Rucellai Palace - 12) All Saints' Church.

From Piazza della Signoria, we proceed by way of Via dei Calzaiuoli to the

CHURCH OF ORSANMICHELE

This takes its name from the earlier church of **St. Michael in the Garden,** which was replaced in 1290 by the Grain Market, the work of Arnolfo di Cambio. This was burnt down in 1304 and rebuilt in 1337 by Francesco Talenti, Neri di Fioravantí and Benci di Cione; subsequently, in 1380, Simone Talenti assigned it for use as a church. The same architects added another floor to the building, to serve as a storehouse for grain; in 1569 it was turned into a Record Office.

The Church has some remarkable features: in shape, it is a huge parallelepiped, the lower part of which consists of covered arcades by Simone Talenti, which he decorated with elaborate three-mullioned windows, purely Gothic in style. Between the arcades, there is a series of tabernacles with statues of the patron saints of the most important Florentine « Guilds ».

CHURCH OF ORSANMICHELE: Interior

INTERIOR: Rectangular in shape, it is unique in being divided into two aisles by large pilasters supporting round arches: it is completely covered with fresco paintings dedicated to the patron saints of the Lesser Guilds.

In the right aisle, the fine **Tabernacle by Orcagna:** painting, sculpture, architecture and colour merge wonderfully to form one of the most remarkable compositions of the florid Gothic style.

PALAZZO DELL'ARTE DELLA LANA

This is in Via dell'Arte della Lana and is joined on to the Church of Orsanmichele by a bridge. It was the seat of one of the richest and most powerful corporations which, at the time of its greatest splendour, numbered more than 30,000 workers, 200 establishments and 20 factories. It was built in 1308 and restored in 1905; it is now the seat of the Dante Society.

LOGGIA OF THE NEW MARKET

From Palazzo dell'Arte della Lana, we take Via Calimala and, after the junction with Via Porta Rossa, we come to the **Loggia of the New Market.** Built between 1547 and 1551, by G. B. Del Tasso, its late Renaissance style is characterised by restrained elegance. Merchants and bankers used to meet here. The small round slab in the centre marks the spot where in the Middle Ages, the « Deals » were signed after battle, and, in Renaissance times, fraudulent bankrupts were put in the pillory and beaten.

Loggia of the New Market

PALAZZO DAVANZATI

Leaving the Loggia of the New Market, and going along Via Pelliceria, we come to Palazzo Davanzati, a nobleman's residence of the 14th century. The upper loggia was added in the 15th century.

The interior is also of interest, where the original furniture has been re-arranged and completely restored.

The Palace contains the Museum of the Florentine House, which offers a complete survey of 15th and 16th century furnishing.

PALAZZO DI PARTE GUELFA

Behind the Loggia of the New Market, stands the Palazzo di Parte Guelfa, in the little square named after it.

The building goes back to the 14th century and was enlarged in the 15th by Filippo Brunelleschi; Vasari completed it in 1589.

In the area where stand these palaces and the Loggia of the « New Market », there are still ancient 13th century houses with towers, the strongholds of the most powerful Florentine families.

CHURCH OF THE HOLY APOSTLES

In the area between Via Por San Maria, Lungarno Acciaioli and Borgo Santi Apostoli (which is also the medieval centre of the city), stands the Church of the Holy Apostles.

Legend has it that it was commissioned by Charlemagne, but in reality it was built at the close of the 11th century on the remains of some ancient Roman baths, probably where stood a children's cemetery called the « Limbo ».

Transformed in the 15th and 16th century, and restored still more recently, it still has some of its original Romanesque features, with remains of 14th century fresco paintings. The doorway is attributed to Benedetto da Rovezzano (16th century).

INTERIOR: this is very picturesque, on the plan of a Basilica with three aisles, separated by a series of columns of green Prato marble, after the Tuscan-Romanesque style, which exercised a decisive influence on the development of Florentine architecture.

CHURCH OF THE HOLY TRINITY

By Borgo Santi Apostoli, we come to **Piazza Santa Trinità,** where stands the church of that name. The building, originally erected in the 11th century for the Vallombrosian monks was later transformed and enlarged in the 13th and 14th century.

The Baroque FAÇADE is attributed to Bernardo Buontalenti (1593-94).

INTERIOR: is one of the first examples of Florentine Gothic: its ground-plan is in the shape of an Egyptian cross (T-shaped), divided into three aisles by large pilasters surmounted by pointed arches and cross-vaults. The side chapels were added in the 14th century.

Spini-Ferroni - Palace

INTERNAL FAÇADE: remains of the previous church can be seen, and fragments of the 14th century fresco painting of the Trinity by Neri di Bicci.

CRYPT: access to this is by the stairs in the middle of the centre aisle; the remains of the ancient Romanesque church can be seen here.

Some interesting palaces are likewise situated in Piazza di Santa Trinità.

PALAZZO BUONDELMONTI at no. 2, built in the 13th century, but transformed in the 15th century; PALAZZO BARTOLINI, at no. 1, built by Baccio d'Agnolo, and the crenellated PALAZZO SPINI-FERRONI, on the far side of Piazza Santa Trinità. It is a fine building, dating from the Middle Ages (1289).

BRIDGE OF THE HOLY TRINITY

Designed and built by Bartolomeo Ammannati, in 1570, it was a wonderful piece of engineering, with its slender elegance. After its destruction in the last war, it was faithfully rebuilt, according to the original design, making use of all the fragments that could be found.

60

Strozzi - Palace ➤

Bridge of the Holy Trinity

PALAZZO STROZZI

This masterpiece of Renaissance architecture bears witness to the splendour and magnificence of the Florence of the period; it was the most important cultural, financial and artistic centre of the city. Begun by Benedetto da Maiano in 1489 for Filippo Strozzi, it was continued by Cronaca until 1504, when the work was interrupted before the rear part was completed.

It is a three-storey building, completely covered with ashlar rustic stone, slightly diminishing in size towards the top.

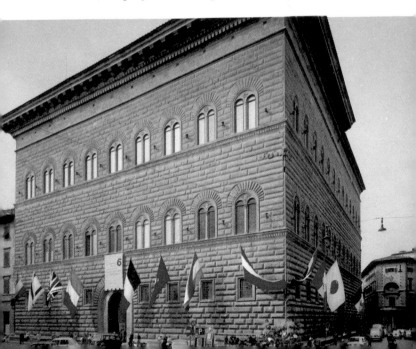

The wrought-iron lanterns and brackets which decorate the sides of the palace are very interesting: they are the work of Caparra, executed to the designs of Benedetto da Maiano and Cronaca. The elegant courtyard with two arcades, one above the other, is also by Cronaca. The building is now the seat of the « Centre for Renaissance Studies » and of the famous « Vieusseux Cabinet », a cultural society founded in 1841 by Vieusseux and attended by illustrious men of letters such as Leopardi, Manzoni and others. Every year, important congresses, and exhibitions of paintings and antiques are held here.

PALAZZO RUCELLAI

From Palazzo Strozzi, on the side of Via Tornabuoni, we follow Via Vigna Nuova until we reach Palazzo Rucellai.

It was built by Bernardo Rossellino (1446-51) to the design of Leon Battista Alberti.

It has three storeys, covered with smooth ashlar and articulated by three orders of parastas and elegant mullioned windows.

CHURCH OF OGNISSANTI

Built in 1251, it was completely reconstructed in 1627 by Bartolomeo Pettirossi.

The Baroque façade of 1637, by Nigetti, was restored in recent times. Above the doorway there is an enamelled terracotta of the Coronation of the Virgin attributed to Benedetto Buglioni. The Romanesque Campanile dates from the 13th century.

The INTERIOR has a nave and transept, almost entirely decorated in the Baroque period.

CHURCH OF OGNISSANTI

Square of the Santissima Annunziata

ITINERARY VI

**1) Square of the « SS. Annunziata » and Ospedale degli Inno-
centi - 2) Church of the SS. Annunziata - 3) Archaeological
Museum - 4) Gallery of the Academy - 5) Church of San Marco
- 6) Museum of San Marco and Fra Angelico - 7) Palazzo Medici-Riccardi and Medici Museum - 8) Church of S. Lorenzo,
Cloister of S. Lorenzo, the Laurentian Library and the Medici
Chapels - 9) Church of Santa Maria Novella.**

SQUARE OF THE SANTISSIMA ANNUNZIATA

From the left of the apse of the Cathedral of Santa Maria
del Fiore, by way of Via dei Servi, we come to the **Square of the
Santissima Annunziata.**

It is a wonderful example of the balanced and measured
harmony of the Renaissance. On three sides, the square is surrounded by arcades:

on the left: the portico of the Confraternity of the « Servants
of Mary », by Antonio da Sangallo and Baccio d'Agnolo (1525);

in the centre: the portico of the Church of the Annunciation,
by Cassini (1501);

on the right: the portico of the Ospedale degli Innocenti;

in the middle: statue of the Grand Duke Ferdinand I, by
Giambologna.

Between the portico of the Confraternity and Via dei Servi,
stands **Palazzo Riccardi Mannelli**, built by Ammannati in 1557.

OSPEDALE DEGLI INNOCENTI

Begun in 1419 by Filippo Brunelleschi, this building is generally considered as the revolutionary introduction to a new
epoch. For the first time, in the early 15th century, we find an

63

architecture well defined within its space, capable of being accurately measured by the human eye, and one which, above all in the proportions of its arcades and vaults, repeats the precise shape of a cube.

The medallions between the arches are the work of Andrea della Robbia (1463) and represent infants in swaddling clothes, foundlings for whom the Hospital was established.

On the right is the entrance to the **Picture Gallery,** a small collection of works of varying importance. Among the most notable are:

3rd Room: pictures by Domenico Ghirlandaio

Adoration of the Magi (Domenico Ghirlandaio)

4th Room: devoted to Luca della Robbia

The Madonna of the Innocents with Child, unrolling a scroll Tabernacle by Della Robbia showing « Madonna with Child and Saints ».

In this room there is also an incomplete manuscript of the Divine Comedy.

CHURCH OF THE ANNUNCIATION

Commissioned by the Order of the « Servants of Mary », and founded by seven young noblemen who wished to withdraw from the world of their day, it was completely reconstructed between 1444 and 1481 by Michelozzo, and again remodelled in the Baroque period.

Through the central doorway, we enter the CLOISTER OF THE VOWS, or atrium, built by Antonio Manetti who adopted a design by Michelozzo.

The walls are covered with interesting paintings, among which are the following:

The Visitation (1516) by Pontormo; The Birth of the Virgin (1514) by Andrea del Sarto; The Adoration of the Magi (Andrea del Sarto). The Nativity (Baldovinetti).

The INTERIOR consists of a nave with side-chapels. Its appearance is decidedly Baroque owing to the sumptuous decoration executed between 1644 and 1790. The ceiling, likewise Baroque, was carved by Giambelli (1644-69) to the design of Volterrano.

On entering the Church, we immediately see on the right, the SMALL MARBLE SANCTUARY: This was built by Lupo Portigiani, after the design of Michelozzo, to preserve the miraculous picture of the Annunciation (painted by an angel, according to legend).

To the left of the portico of Santa Annunziata, is the entrance to the

CLOISTER OF THE DEAD, likewise designed by Michelozzo, and built by Pagno Portigiani. Here we admire:

Stories of the « Servants of Mary », by Poccetti and Matteo Rosselli; « Madonna del Sacco », lunette at the far end and a famous work by Andrea del Sarto.

Leaving the church and facing away from it, we turn on

the left into Via Colonna, where, at no. 38 stands the Archaeological Museum.

ARCHAEOLOGICAL MUSEUM

a very important one, one of the largest and richest in Italy
and the world. It contains the Etruscan and Egyptian Museums.

GROUND FLOOR: Collection of Greco-Roman and Etruscan
sculpture. In some 50 rooms, it contains statues, objects and
fragments brought to light in excavations. In the first rooms, Greco-Roman works.

In Room 8, begins the TOPOGRAPHICAL MUSEUM OF ETRU-
RIA with artistic documentation of the Etruscan civilisation from
the 8th to the 1st century B.C. The collection is divided by
cities.

In the GARDEN many reconstructed Etruscan tombs and monuments.

1st FLOOR: EGYPTIAN MUSEUM: This is the largest and
richest, apart from those of Turin and London.

In its eight rooms are displayed sculptures, inscriptions,
papyruses, monuments, stelae, tombs and mummies.

ETRUSCAN, GREEK AND ROMAN ANTIQUARIUM: this is
housed in Rooms 9-12. It is an interesting collection of sculptures, bronzes and precious objects belonging to the three civilisations.

NUMISMATIC COLLECTION (Rooms 15, 16, 17, 18): this is
a valuable collection of Italian coins of every period, from the
most ancient Etruscan, Greek and Roman pieces to those of
the early Middle Ages. Among the most interesting are the
« aes grave » and the « aes rude » of Latium and Etruria.

COLLECTION OF PRECIOUS OBJECTS (Rooms 19, 20): In
the glass cases in these two rooms are displayed jewellery,
gold and silver of the ancient civilisations.

GALLERY OF THE ACADEMY

This is situated in Via Ricasoli, into which we turn from Piazza S. Marco; at no. 52. In addition to a fine picture gallery, it
has some of Michelangelo's most important sculptures.

From the entrance, we reach the long corridor, where are
displayed:
4 Prisoners (1518) sculpted by Michelangelo for the tomb of
Julius II, which was never carried out to the original plan. Although the statues are meant to be merely rough casts, they
can be considered as complete. Indeed, it is precisely this
« unfinished » technique which accounts for some of the great
artist's most powerful and dramatic creations.
St. Matthew, likewise unfinished. The Palestrina Pietà (1515-20),
one of Michelangelo's most significant works: the unfinished
state, the pyramidal composition and the emaciated forms create the dramatic effect of the subject in all its intensity.

David (1501-1504); this stands in front of the end wall,
also called « Tribuna del David ». It is a very famous statue,
obtained with consummate skill from an imperfect block of

ACADEMY - David (Michelangiolo)

ACADEMY - Pietà di Palestrina (Michelangiolo)

marble, which Michelangelo himself called « spoilt ». Although in its pose the statue follows the classical models, it combines within itself not only the artist's particular vision but also that of the whole Renaissance, a serene vision of the hero, the man who stands sure of himself in the world he is about to conquer. David's beautiful face, so proud in the firm lines of the profile and in the intense gaze, the agile and alert body, the stupendous hand grasping the stone, so well observed in the bundles of veins and nerves running across it — all this expresses the strength, determination and nobility of man, the firm will of the hero. On the walls, tapestries of the 16th, 17th and 18th century.

PICTURE GALLERY: minor Florentine artists of the 12th to the 16th century, are represented here. Among the most important are:

1st Room: Mary Magdalene and scenes from her life, by the « Maestro della Maddalena ».

2nd Room: Works by Agnolo Gaddi, and a Pietà by Giovanni da Milano.

3rd Room: « Stories of Christ »; by Taddeo Gaddi.

7th Room: « The Adimari Wedding » painted on a wedding chest by an unknown artist.

There are also various works by Lorenzo Monaco.

We would mention also works by Bernardo Daddi, Neri di Bicci, Cosimo Rosselli, Filippino Lippi, Fra' Bartolomeo, Paolo Uccello and Andrea del Castagno.

CHURCH OF SAN MARCO

From the Gallery of the Academy, we proceed along Via Ricasoli, on the right and soon reach Piazza San Marco with the Church and Convent of San Marco. The Church was built in the 13th century, and altered in 1437 by Michelozzo and again in 1687 by P. F. Silvani. The façade is by Gioacchino Pronti (1780); it repeats the basic elements of Baroque architecture, but in a restrained and balanced style.

MUSEUM OF SAN MARCO or OF FRA ANGELICO

This is housed in the ancient Convent of San Marco, rebuilt by Michelozzo in 1437, to the order of Cosimo the Elder, on the site of the old monastery of the Vallombrosian monks.

In 1866, the Convent was suppressed, arranged as a Museum and devoted to Fra' Angelico.

Fra' Angelico is one of the most enigmatic personalities in Italian art. His style seems to fluctuate between the two extremes of an ascetic vision of the medieval type and a plastic and spatial conception derived straight from Masaccio. In fact, these contrasting tendencies find their harmony in a serene art expressed in compositions of limpid clarity and in modest, unassuming tones.

Immediately to the right of the entrance, we find the PILGRIM'S HOSTEL. This contains numerous paintings on wood by Fra Angelico which provide an exhaustive documentation of his development as an artist.

Among the finest and most important of these, we would mention:

The Linen-Weavers' Tabernacle; Madonna with Child and Saints; The Coronation of the Virgin; 35 Stories from the Life of Christ and of the Virgin; « The Madonna of the Star »; The Annunciation; The Last Judgment.

ROOM OF THE LAVABO: with works by Fra Bartolomeo.

LARGE REFECTORY: with works by Fra Bartolomeo, Sogliani and Albertinelli.

Returning to the Cloister, we come to the

CHAPTER HOUSE: here is the large fresco painting of the Crucifixion by Fra Angelico.

ST. MARCO - Annunciation (Beato Angelico)

Across the corridor (entrance opposite to that of the Cloister), we come to the 2nd cloister. The door on the right of the corridor leads to the first floor. At the foot of the stairs, is the

SMALL REFECTORY: where we admire Domenico Ghirlandaio's « Last Supper », similar to the one in the Convent of Ognissanti. We proceed to the

1st FLOOR: here are the old cells of the Dominicans, for the most part with frescoes by Fra Angelico and his pupils. Opposite the stairway is the

Annunciation by Fra Angelico. 1st cell: « Noli me tangere » (Fra Angelico). 3rd cell: « The Annunciation », perhaps the finest of Fra Angelico's frescoes. 6th cell: The Transfiguration. 9th cell: The Coronation of the Virgin.

PRIOR'S QUARTERS: where Girolamo Savonarola lived for some time.

Portrait of Savonarola (Fra Bartolomeo); Savonarola's Death at the Stake (Fra Bartolomeo); 31st cell: St. Antonino; 32-33, a double cell, perhaps the one occupied by Fra Angelico; 35th cell: fresco of the « Company of the Apostles »; cells 38 and 39: served as a retreat for Cosimo the Elder: they are decorated with frescoes by Benozzo Gozzoli.

LIBRARY OF THE CONVENT: a beautiful room; the work of Michelozzo (1396-1472), one of the most important artists of the Florentine Renaissance.

In the Library: glass cases contain important documents and illuminated manuscripts.

MEDICI-RICCARDI PALACE

We leave Piazza San Marco and then proceed along Via Cavour until we reach Palazzo Medici-Riccardi.

This, the official residence of the Medici family up to the time of Cosimo I who moved to Palazzo Vecchio, was built between 1444 and 1460 by Michelozzo, to the order of Cosimo the Elder, and later remodelled.

Crossing the elegant courtyard, we reach the MEDICI MUSEUM housed in the apartments of Lorenzo the Magnificent.

MEDICI MUSEUM - Voyage of the Three Kings (B. Gozzoli)

1st Room: this contains Medici tapestries, documents and reproductions concerning the great Florentine family; *2nd Room:* portraits of the Medici; *Passage:* noteworthy, among other exhibits, a « Madonna and Child » by Filippo Lippi; *3rd Room:* more portraits of the Medici by Bronzino, the Court portrait painter. It also contains the death mask of Lorenzo; *4th Room:* Portrait of Cosimo I by Pontormo — small portraits of other members of the Medici family by Bronzino.

In its rooms the glittering court life of Lorenzo the Magnificent and of the many famous men of literature and art of the Florence of this time was carried on, turning it into one of the most fruitful centres of Renaissance civilisation.

CHAPEL: this was built by Michelozzo and was adorned with the large fresco painting of
« The Adoration of the Magi » by Benozzo Gozzoli (1459-1460); simple and fresh in composition, it depicts accurately the costumes of the period and gives portraits of the most notable personalities of the day, from that of Lorenzo the Magnificent to a self-portrait of the artist.

CHURCH OF SAN LORENZO

Immediately after Palazzo Medici-Riccardi, we leave Via Cavour, and turn into Via de' Gori, which leads us to Piazza San Lorenzo. Here stands the Church of San Lorenzo, first built in 393, when it was consecrated by St. Ambrose, Bishop of Milan. It was rebuilt in the Romanesque style in the 11th century. At the orders of the Medici, it was again transformed in 1419 by Brunelleschi and once more between 1442 and 1446. Only in 1460 was it completed by Antonio Manetti.

THE INTERIOR follows the Basilica pattern of the earliest Christian churches, with three aisles, a transept and panelled ceiling. In this setting, Brunelleschi, a superb artist and inter-

CHURCH OF SAN LORENZO

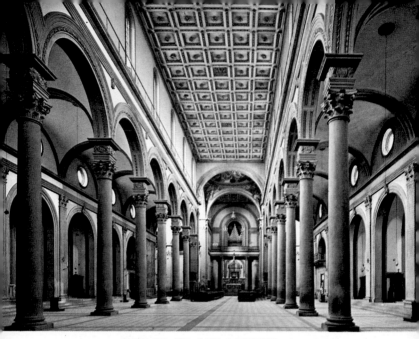

CHURCH OF SAN LORENZO: Interior

preter of the spirit of the Renaissance, created a serene, harmonious space, strictly defined in its parts and emphasised by the functional use of « pietra serena » to bring out the essential framework of the building. The result was one of the loveliest of 15th century Florentine buildings.

The reconstruction of the façade, entrusted to Michelangelo, was never carried out, but he added the New Sacristy and the Laurentian Library.

MAIN CHAPEL: its proportions have now been distorted and diminished by the addition, at the back, of the Chapel of the Princes.

Near the altar, bronze grilles surround the tomb of Cosimo the Elder. Close by is the tomb of Donatello, buried here at his express wish.

OLD SACRISTY: this is reached after the 2nd Chapel in the left arm of the transept. It was built by Filippo Brunelleschi, between 1420 and 1429, and consists of a square room surmounted by a hemispherical dome, with lunettes on each of the four sides. The structures are outlined with strips of « pietra serena » which help to create the clear, precise and harmonious aspect characteristic of Brunelleschi's art.

CLOISTER OF SAN LORENZO: this can be reached from the interior of the Church through the Martelli Chapel, or from the outside, on the left of the façade. It is in the style of Brunelleschi and was built in 1457. On the other side of the Cloister, we go up to the

LAURENTIAN LIBRARY: this can also be reached from the interior of the Church of San Lorenzo.

Begun to the commission of Cosimo the Elder, and enlarged by Lorenzo the Magnificent, it was built in 1524 by Michelangelo. It is interesting not only for its collection of codices, manuscripts and rare books, but also for its architecture. It is indeed one of Michelangelo's most brilliant achievements: the architectural mass is conceived as material to be moulded and enlivened by a continuous series of blind windows and coupled columns. The result is a lively and harmonious plastic whole which finds its marvellous conclusion in the fine and elegant stairway.

THE MEDICI CHAPELS: turning behind the Church of San Lorenzo as far as Piazza Madonna, we come to the entrance to the **Medici Chapels.** They can also be reached from the interior of the Church. Passing the Crypt, with the tombstones of the Medici Princes, we ascend to the great Chapel of the Rulers of Florence.

The building was begun in 1604 by Matteo Nigetti and completed many years later. It has an octagonal ground-plan, surmounted by a cupola which was decorated with fresco paintings by Pietro Benvenuti as late as 1829.

The whole building is completely covered with stone, rare marbles and precious stones which confer upon it an atmosphere of sumptuous majesty, in keeping with the aim of extolling the princely house which was the intention of those who commissioned it.

Along the walls are 6 sarcophagi of Grand Dukes of Tuscany. The two large statues of gilt bronze are by Tacca (17th century).

At the base of the walls are the coats-of-arms of 16 cities of the Grand Duchy.

NEW SACRISTY: this was begun in 1520 by Michelangelo and completed by Vasari in 1557. It is called the « **New Sacristy** » to distinguish it from the « **Old Sacristy** » built by Brunelleschi. The two interiors, seemingly alike (in fact, Michelangelo's is a variation on Brunelleschi's) are nevertheless essentially different: the serenely proportioned space of the Old Sacristy is replaced here by an equally harmonious space, which is, however, given a dynamic movement by means of continuous linking of the surfaces with blind windows, pilaster strips and marked outlines of « pietra serena ».

On the left: tomb of **Lorenzo, Duke of Urbino** (Michelangelo). The two statues on the sarcophagus represent **Dawn** and **Dusk.**

On the right: the tomb of **Giuliano, Duke of Nemours** (also by Michelangelo). The two statues on the sarcophagus represent **Day** and **Night.** In the statue of Day, note the barely outlined face, in contrast with the finish of the rest. Once again, the « unfinished » technique gives an impression of intimate pathos and deeply-felt drama.

SANTA MARIA NOVELLA SQUARE

One of the finest and most spacious squares of Florence. Here the « Palio dei Cocchi » used to take place, a race instituted by Cosimo I, consisting of a chariot race resembling the races of ancient Rome. The ends of the track were marked by the obelisks which still stand there, erected by Giambologna.

Opposite the façade of the beautiful Church of Santa Maria Novella on the other side of the square, is the elegant LOGGIA DI SAN PAOLO, dating from the late 15th century, a good imitation of Brunelleschi's Loggia degli Innocenti in Piazza SS. Annunziata. The terracotta medallions are by Giovanni della Robbia.

MEDICI CHAPEL - Tomb of Lorenzo, Duke of Urbino (Michelangiolo)

CHURCH OF SANTA MARIA NOVELLA

It was begun for the Dominican Order in 1278, to replace a previous small church, and was completed in 1360. The fine Campanile is by Fra Jacopo Talenti. Along the wall adjoining the façade and surrounding the old cemetery are the tombs of noble Florentine families.

FACADE: the lower part dates from the 14th century and follows the traditional Tuscan Romanesque-Gothic style, with decorations of marble in two colours and with a feeling for the precise division of surfaces.

The upper part of the façade is in the Renaissance style, designed by Leon Battista Alberti and completed by Giovanni Bettini (1456-70).

The INTERIOR is in the shape of an Egyptian cross (« T » shape): it has three aisles, separated by pillars supporting pointed arches and cross vaults. Towards the end, the distances between the pillars become slightly smaller, thus creating the illusion of greater depth.

SACRISTY: Built by Jacopo Talenti in 1350: there is an interesting painting of a Crucifix on wood, recently attributed to Giotto.

LEFT AISLE: Also to be noted: (on the right of the entrance) the terracotta lavabo by Giovanni della Robbia; on the end

Church of Santa Maria Novella ➤

MEDICI CHAPELS - Tomb of Giuliano, Duke of Nemours
(Michelangiolo)

CHURCH OF SANTA MARIA NOVELLA: Interior

wall a large cupboard designed by Buontalenti: paintings by
Jacopo Ligozzi, Stradano, as well as a Crucifix by Vasari.

RIGHT AISLE:

Monument to the Blessed Villano (1415) by Rossellino; Chapel
of the « Pura », note the wooden Crucifix.

RIGHT ARM OF TRANSEPT:

3 Gothic tombs: of Bishop Aliotti (Tino di Camaino), of the
monk Aldovrando Cavalcanti (Nino Pisano) and of Giuseppe,
Patriarch of Constantinople; Rucellai Chapel: this is on a higher
level and has 14th century frescoes; Bardi Chapel: frescoes by
Spinello Aretino; Strozzi Chapel: attractive frescoes by Filippino
Lippi; the tomb of Filippo Strozzi is by Benedetto da Maiano.

MAIN CHAPEL:

Easter Candlestick with twisted columns; on the polychrome mar-

SPANISH CHAPEL - Triumph of St. Thomas Aquinas

ble altar (an ugly 17th century addition) a large bronze Crucifix by Giambologna; the Apse is entirely covered with a cycle of frescoes by Domenico Ghirlandaio and many of his pupils (1485-90); on the vault, frescoes by Orcagna have been discovered which are now being restored.

LEFT ARM OF TRANSEPT:
Gondi Chapel: by Giuliano da Sangallo.
On the altar, the wooden Crucifix by Brunelleschi (1503), the only sculpture of his which has come down to us: it was carved to contrast with that by Donatello in the Church of Santa Croce, which Brunelleschi had criticised as being too realistic.

LEFT AISLE:
opposite the last pillar but one, one of Masaccio's masterpieces: the « Holy Trinity » (1428).

LARGE SPANISH CHAPEL: built in 1350 by Jacopo Talenti as the Chapter House of the Convent, about 1540 it became the Chapel of Eleanor of Toledo. It is entirely decorated with frescoes by Andrea di Firenze glorifying the Dominican Order.

ENTRANCE WALL: Stories of the life, martyrdom and miracles of St. Peter the Martyr.

OPPOSITE WALL: Stories of the Passion.

RIGHT WALL: « The Church Militant »: a large fresco painting, one of the artist's most famous works. Starting from the bottom, it shows the Glory of the Dominicans, from their preaching to the conversions brought about by them and to the final vision of Christ in Paradise.

LEFT WALL: « Triumph of St. Thomas of Aquinas ».

77

PONTE VECCHIO

ITINERARY VII

1) Old Bridge - 2) Pitti Palace: a) Palatine Gallery; b) Museum « degli Argenti »; c) Gallery of Modern Art - 3) Boboli Gardens - 4) Church of the Holy Spirit - 5) Carmine Church.

From Piazza della Signoria, we take Via Por San Maria to reach the picturesque

PONTE VECCHIO

So called because it is the city's oldest bridge. It was built around 1350 probably by Neri di Fioravante, on the spot where, until a few years before, had stood a 10th century wooden bridge, swept away in 1333 by the Arno in flood.

The characteristic rows of shops on either side, reserved by Ferdinand I exclusively for goldsmiths, have been a distinctive feature of the bridge since that time, giving it not only an appearance and function all its own, but also, unique charm and local colour.

The back-shops and dwellings of the goldsmiths, projecting over the river, complete the picturesque aspect of this bridge, giving the impression that the city extends above the river. Above the houses on one side runs Vasari's Corridor, which, as already mentioned, connects Palazzo Vecchio and the Uffizi Gallery to Palazzo Pitti.

In the middle of the bridge, under the arches which look out onto the Arno, there is a statue by Romanelli of Benvenuto Cellini, the greatest 16th century Florentine goldsmith.

PALAZZO PITTI

From Ponte Vecchio, we go along Via Guicciardini to Piazza Pitti where stands the magnificent palace built for the powerful Florentine banker, Luca Pitti, who jealously contended the supremacy of the Medici and plotted against them. Reprieved, after having been condemned to death, he left the Palace, which was bought by Cosimo I. When the Medici family died out, it passed to the House of Lorraine, and later, from 1855 to 1871, was the residence of the Royal House of Savoy.

Brunelleschi planned the building but it was started by Luca Fancelli in 1458. After being acquired by Cosimo I and Eleanor of Toledo, it was enlarged between 1558 and 1577 by Ammannati.

PALATINE GALLERY

This is reached through the arch on the left of Palazzo Pitti and then through the door immediately on the right.

The large and interesting collection was begun by Cosimo II in 1620 and constantly added to by the Medici family and later by the House of Lorraine. The works are arranged without any regard for schools or chronology, with a view to ornamental effect only, according to the taste of the Seventeenth Century Court.

Beyond the wide **Staircase** and the **Vestibule** we reach the **Porphyry Cup Room** (which connects Palazzo Pitti with the Uffizi Gallery means of a long corridor). We next enter

PITTI PALACE

PALATINE GALLERY - Room of the Iliad

ROOM 1: Room of THE ILIAD: in the centre, the statue of Charity by Bartolini (1524).
Pregnant Woman (1506) by Raphael; The Assumption of the Virgin (Andrea del Sarto); Portrait of a Woman (Ridolfo del Ghirlandaio), inspired by Raphael's « Pregnant Woman »; Portrait of Diego Mendoza, by Titian; The Assumption, by Andrea del Sarto; Portrait of Waldemar Christian of Denmark, by Sustermans; Portrait of Philip IV, by Velasquez.

ROOM II, ROOM OF SATURN: On the ceiling, frescoes representing Saturn, by Ciro Ferri, to the design of Pietro da Cortona, one of the 17th century' painters most renowned for decorating walls and ceilings in a manner rightly called « trompe l'oeil ». His art, however, never degenerates into the trite rhetoric of the Baroque, in spite of certain touches of virtuosity, but is full of vitality and luminous freshness.
The Madonna of the Grand Duke (Raphael: 1504-05); Disputation on the Trinity (Andrea del Sarto: 1517); Portrait of the Doni Couple (Raphael); The Madonna of the Canopy (Raphael: 1506); The Descent from the Cross (Perugino); Mary Magdalene (Perugino); The Madonna della Seggiola (Raphael: 1515): an important work, not only because it shows the artist in his full maturity, but also for the human warmth that emanates from the Madonna and Child.

80

PALATINE GALLERY - Madonna of the Chair (Raphael)

ROOM III, ROOM OF JUPITER: (on the ceiling, an allegory of Jupiter, by Pietro da Cortona and Ferri).
St. John the Baptist (Andrea del Sarto: 1523); Descent from the Cross (Fra Bartolomeo: 1516); Nymphs and Satyrs (Paul Rubens); The Annunciation (Andrea del Sarto); The Woman with a Veil (Raphael): it is perhaps a portrait of the Fornarina.

ROOM IV: ROOM OF MARS: here also the paintings on the ceiling are by Pietro da Cortona (1646).
Madonna and Child (Murillo); The Four Philosophers (Rubens): in this picture, the artist portrays himself and his brother conversing with the philosophers Gustus Lipsius and Jan Van Der Wouwer; Portrait of Daniele Barbaro (Veronese); Portrait of Cardinal Bentivoglio (a masterpiece by Van Dyck); Luigi Cornaro (Tintoretto).

ROOM V, ROOM OF APOLLO:
Portrait of a Nobleman (Titian: 1540): this is one of the artist's finest and most important works; Mary Magdalene (Titian); ·The Holy Family (Andrea del Sarto).

ROOM VI, ROOM OF VENUS:
La Bella (Titian), perhaps a portrait of Eleanor of Urbino; Portrait of Pietro Aretino, another portrait by Titian; Concert: (Giorgione, or, according to others, Titian); Several paintings by Rubens.

81

ROOM VII, CASTAGNOLI ROOM: decorated in the 19th century, by the artist whose name it bears.

In the centre, a beautiful table, inlaid with stones.

ROOM VIII, ROOM OF VOLTERRANO'S ALLEGORIES:
Prank of the Parish Priest, Arlotto (Volterrano).

ROOM IX, ROOM OF THE FINE ARTS: works by Cigoli.

ROOM X, ROOM OF HERCULES: Sèvres Vase.

ROOM XI, ROOM OF DAWN: works by Empoli and Lorenzo Lippi.

ROOM XII, ROOM OF BERENICE: works by Salvator Rosa.

ROOM VIII, ROOM OF THE DRUMS: so-called after the shape of the seats. Contains the famous « St. Sebastian » by Sodoma
Here begins the old Palatine Gallery containing the first 500 pieces of the Medici Collection.

PALATINE GALLERY - The Woman with a Veil (Raphael)

ROOM XIX, ROOM OF PROMETHEUS:

Madonna and Child (Filippo Lippi); Dance of Apollo and the Muses (Giulio Romano).

ROOM XX, POCETTI GALLERY: so-called after the painter who decorated it:

2 Portraits (Rubens); Self-portrait by Salvator Rosa; St. Jerome (showing the influence of Caravaggio).

ROOM XXI, CORRIDOR OF THE COLUMNS: with Flemish paintings.

ROOM XXII, ROOM OF JUSTICE:

Portraits of Men (Tintoretto); Portrait of a Man (Titian); Portrait (Veronese); The Redeemer (Tintoretto); The Saviour (Titian).

ROOM XXIII, ROOM OF FLORA:

Portrait of Tommaso Mosti (Titian); Venus Italica (in the centre); by Antonio Canova; Stories ef Joseph the Jew (A. del Sarto); The Adoration of the Magi (Pontormo).

ROOM XXIV, ROOM OF THE CHERUBS: paintings of the sea, hunting scenes, flowers and fruit by Rachel Ruysch and Henrik Gubbels.

Young girl with Candle (Schalken).

ROOM XXV, ROOM OF ULYSSES:

The Madonna d'Impannata (Raphael 1514); Portrait of Andrea Frizier (Tintoretto); Ecce Homo (Cigoli); Works by Guido Reni and Tintoretto.

ROOM XXVI, BATH ROOM: and attractive room in the neo-classical style.

ROOM XXVII, ROOM OF THE EDUCATION OF JUPITER:

Cupid Sleeping (by Caravaggio); Judith (Allori).

ROOM XVIII, ROOM OF THE STOVE: on the walls, frescoes by Pietro da Cortona.

Returning to Room VI, the Room of Venus, we proceed to the

FORMER ROYAL APARTMENTS

consisting of a series of fine and sumptuous rooms, once reserved for the use of the Kings of Italy.

MUSEUM « DEGLI ARGENTI »

This is on the ground floor and contains a very complete collection of jewellery, precious stones, various valuable objects, cameos, fabrics, carpets and china.

GALLERY OF MODERN ART

This is on the second floor. Founded in 1860, it has been

BOBOLI GARDENS - « Bacchino »

constantly enlarged and enriched with 19th and 20th century works of the Tuscan School.

In Room XIX are works by the Florentine impressionist painters who contributed to the revival of Italian painting in the 20th century.

Room XX is devoted to Fattori, the greatest exponent of the Florentine impressionist school.

THE BOBOLI GARDENS

These are on the slopes of the Boboli hill and, as we have already mentioned, they continue the architecture of Palazzo Pitti. It is one of the happiest artistic creations, in which architecture, sculpture and nature seem to merge into a marvellous unity. The work, commissioned by Eleanor of Toledo in 1550, was begun by Tribolo, and continued and brought to completion by Ammannati and others.

84

Through the GATE OF BACCHUS in the arcade on the left, we reach the large square.

Here, immediately on the left, is the famous **« Bacchino »** a small fountain consisting of a tortoise surmounted by a fat little dwarf. This represents the famous dwarf of Cosimo I, Pietro Barbino.

We proceed (along the corridor designed by Vasari to join Palazzo Pitti to the Uffizi Gallery) until we reach.

BUONTALENTI'S GROTTO: (1583). This consists of three parts, with statues representing:

Ceres and Apollo (Baccio Bandinelli); Prisoners (copies of Michelangelo's originals); Venus leaving her Bath (Giambologna).

An avenue on the right leads to the **Amphitheatre** of the 17th-18th century.

We climb still further up, to **« Neptune's Fishpond »** a large pool above which stand statues of sirens and of the God Neptune.

The lanes of the **Belvedere** are also picturesque and attractive. Still higher up, we come to the **« Garden of the Cavalier »** with the ancient bastion built by Michelangelo for the ˙defence of the city. We go down again on the left till we reach the **Aviary Meadow,** whence, by way of the « Grand Avenue », flanked by pines and cypresses, we reach the « Island ». In the middle

BOBOLI GARDENS - Amphitheatre

Church of the Holy Spirit (Santo Spirito)

of this stands the Fountain of the Ocean, by Giambologna, with a statue of Ocean in the centre (the original is in Bargello) surrounded by representations of the most important rivers in the world.

CHURCH OF THE HOLY SPIRIT

From Piazza Felice, we turn into Via Mazzetta which brings us to Piazza Santo Spirito.

The Church is the last work by Brunelleschi (1444). The very plain, unadorned façade leaves us unprepared for the beauty of the interior.

The INTERIOR is in the shape of a Latin cross, with three aisles. Brunelleschi's great art here reaches its summit: the precisely defined space, easily comprehended by the eye in all its parts, and strictly proportioned, which we have already admired in the Church of San Lorenzo (likewise by Brunelleschi) is here filled with a new vitality. In fact, a series of semi-circular chapels, all alike, enlivens the whole perimeter without interruption, while in its turn, an unbroken row of columns follows the four arms of the Church.

Also of interest are the **Vestibule by Cronaca** (1492-94), the **Sacristy** designed by Giuliano da Sangallo (1489-92) and the **Refectory** with frescoes by Orcagna.

THE CARMINE CHURCH

From Piazza Santo Spirito, we follow Via Sant'Agostino and, after the junction with Via Serragli, Via S. Monaca, until we reach Piazza del Carmine, where stands the Church of that name.

Begun in 1268, in the Romanesque-Gothic style, it was enlarged and altered several times in later periods. After the fire of 1771, which destroyed the greater part of the building, leaving only the Corsini and Brancacci Chapels, it was rebuilt in recent times.

The INTERIOR is in the shape of a Latin cross, and the

The Expulsion of Adam and Eve from Paradise

ceiling is decorated in the Baroque style.

BRANCACCI CHAPEL: this is at the end of the right arm of the transept and contains a cycle of frescoes which are among the most significant and revolutionary works of Italian art on the threshold of the Renaissance. The frescoes, begun in 1424-25 by Masolino da Panicale, a painter in the Gothic tradition and Masaccio's teacher, were continued by Masaccio himself (1426-27) who here created his masterpiece.

The various Stories are divided in panels and arranged in accordance with strict rules of perspective: these, however, are not mere learned abstractions, but veritable creations of real space, bound up with the actual position of the panels, the natural light in the Chapel, and the treatment of the scenes. In this kind of composition the figures of Christ, the Saints and Angels lose all vestiges of mysticism and become the expression of a moody, pensive humanity. The frescoes in the Chapel are arranged as follows

1) The Expulsion of Adam and Eve (M); 2) The Tribute Money (M); 3) St. Peter Preaching (m); 4) St. Peter baptizing converts (M); 5) The Healing of the Lame Man (M); 6) St. Peter raises Tabitha (mM); 7) The Temptation of Adam and Eve (m); 8) St. Paul visits St. Peter in Prison (FL); 9) St. Peter raises the Emperor's Nephew (FL); 10) St. Peter Enthroned (M); 11) St. Peter heals the sick with his shadow (M); 12) St. Peter and St. John giving alms (M); 13) The Crucifixion of St. Peter (FL); 14) St. Peter and St. Paul before the pro-consul (FL); 15) The Angel frees St. Peter (FL).

M = Masaccio   m = Masolino
FL = Filippino Lippi   87

ENVIRONS

1) Piazzale Michelangelo; 2) San Miniato al Monte; 3) Belvedere Fortress; 4) Certosa del Galluzzo; 5) Fiesole: a) Abbey of Fiesole; b) Archaeological Area; c) San Francesco di Fiesole; d) Cathedral.

PIAZZALE MICHELANGELO

After crossing the Ponte Vecchio, we proceed along Lungarno Torrigiani and Lungarno Serristori as far as **Porta San Nicolò,** where the hill leading up to **Piazzale Michelangelo** begins.

From here, the view over the city has something magical about it. From the Piazzale, we can enjoy a stupendous panorama of Florence, with the Arno flowing through it, with its bridges, towers, campaniles and domes, and the beautiful hills surrounding it, as far as those of Fiesole in the distance, which are opposite the Piazzale. In the centre stands the monument to Michelangelo, consisting of a copy of his David, and bronze reproductions of the four statues of the Medici Tombs, his marvellous sculptures in Florence. From Piazzale Michelangelo, we climb up to San Miniato al Monte. On the way, the 16th century church of **San Salvatore al Monte** merits a brief inspection: because of its beauty. Michelangelo himself called it his « lovely country-girl ».

CHURCH OF SAN MINIATO AL MONTE

It was built in 1080 on the site of a previous church to the order of Bishop Hildebrand.

The Romanesque style which we admired in the Baptistery of St. John, interpreted with the original refinement so typical of Florentine architecture, finds in this church a similar and equally successful style. Again decoration in marble of two colours is applied to convey a sense of clearly defined volumes to the observer while at the same time it confers upon the whole a note of picturesque intimacy.

The INTERIOR: has three aisles and still preserves its original aspect almost intact. Restorations made in the 19th century have spoilt the delicate colour scheme of the marbles, by applying imitation « scagliola » to the columns.

The CENTRE AISLE has a beautiful floor with the signs of the Zodiac and other symbols. In the centre, is the **Chapel of the Crucifix,** by Michelozzo, (1488), so called because it was built to house the Crucifix of San Giovanni Gualberto, now in the Church of the Holy Trinity. On the altar: a painting on wood by Agnolo Gaddi with stories of San Miniato, S. Giovanni Gualberto, the Annunciation and stories of the Passion.

Right Aisle: here there are ancient frescoes: **The Sacristy** walls have been decorated by Spinello Aretino with stories of St. Benedict (1387).

Left Aisle: we go down the presbytery stairs and come to the **Chapel of the Cardinal of Portugal,** built for James, Archbishop of Lisbon, who died in 1459. In it are summed up the main lines of Renaissance art. It is the work of Antonio Manetti (a pupil of Brunelleschi) who in this rectangular space follows the great master's style. Luca della Robbia is responsible for the decoration of the five tondos, while the sarcophagus is by Antonio Rossellino. Pollaiolo and Baldovinetti also collaborated.

CHURCH OF SAN MINIATO AL MONTE

CHURCH OF SAN MINIATO AL MONTE - Interior

To the left of the Church of San Miniato rises the massive sixteenth century Campanile.

Campanile: During the siege by the Imperial troops in 1530, Michelangelo used it as a fortification. It was in fact from here that he fired the guns to bombard the enemy forces, protecting the bell tower at the same time by embankments and other means of protection (and indeed the Campanile suffured no damage).

To the right of the Church stands the BISHOPS' PALACE with fine mullioned windows on the 1st floor. It was begun in the 13th century and completed in the 14th, and was the summer residence of the bishops of Florence.

BELVEDERE FORTRESS

Descending by way of Viale Galileo, we find on the right, before reaching the Piazzale, Via San Leonardo. This steep, winding and picturesque road affords us every now and then

Certosa del Galluzzo (Carthusian Monastery)

wide views over Florence and brings us to Porta S. Giorgio, immediately after which we find, on the left, the entrance to the Fortress, above the Boboli Gardens. This Fortress, which was built by Giovanni de' Medici and Buontalenti at the command of Ferdinand I, houses an art exhibition and is also used for cultural and tourist attractions.

From the huge glacis below the main building, a fine view of Florence is obtained.

CERTOSA DEL GALLUZZO
(Carthusian Monastery)

Leaving Florence by the Porta Romana, after some 5 kms we reach the village of Galluzzo, and beyond this, on a hill thickly covered with olives and cypresses, we arrive at the **Certosa del Galluzzo.** It was built in 1341 at the command of Nicola Acciaiuoli and was subsequently enlarged and remodelled; recently it was again restored in order to repair the damage suffered during the Second World War.

A long flight of steps brings us to the little square where stands the **Church of San Lorenzo,** the façade of which dates from the second half of the 16th century.

The INTERIOR is divided transversely into two parts, in accordance with the tradition of the Carthusian monks; the front part for the lay brothers, and the rear part for the monks.

Chapel of the Blessed Virgin, in the shape of a Greek cross, built for Cardinal Agnolo Acciaiuoli.

We return to the Chapel of the Virgin and enter the **Rear Part** of the Church, reserved for the monks. Here there are very fine inlaid wooden stalls, and on the walls, frescoes by Poccetti.

THE CASCINE

It is very extensive (one of the largest in Italy) and consists of a series of long avenues and green lawns. It was once an estate of the Medici: in the 18 th century it became the property of the Municipality as a public park. It is now still more attractive because of its sports installations: in addition to tennis courts and swimming pools, it has tracks for triding and gallopping.

◀ Belvedere Fortress

FIESOLE

Climbing up the hill to Fiesole, on the right of the Arno, we come to the ancient cathedral of the little town, the **Abbey Church of Fiesole** which, from 1028 to 1437, belonged to the Benedictines. The façade, in the Romanesque style, is very similar to the almost contemporary one of San Miniato al Monte and was never finished.

The interior, however, in the shape of a Latin cross, and with one aisle only, was built in the Renaissance period. We then reach the little town of Fiesole which represents the most ancient centre of Etruscan civilisation in the area. This later expanded towards the Arno where another centre was established, later enlarged by the Romans and given the name of Florentia. Indeed, behind the apse of the Cathedral at Fiesole, extends the **Archaelogical Area** full of Etruscan antiquities. Nearby there is also a **Roman Theatre** dating from the 1st century B.C. and the **Baths** likewise of the 1st century B.C. Fiesole has some fine artistic works.

THE CATHEDRAL

Begun in 1028 and enlarged later, it is in the Romanesque style, simple and unadorned.

The interior has three aisles, separated by columns surmounted by irregular round arches and a bare wall.

As in San Miniato, the apse is on a higher level, to allow for the crypt. In the Presbytery, the **Salutati Chapel** is of interest with the tomb of Bishop Leonardo Salutati and his bust, a remarkable work by Mino da Fiesole. Among other monuments of interest, we point out the BISHOP'S PALACE (near the Cathedral) and above all one of the most picturesque places in the environs of Florence.

FIESOLE - The Cathedral and Roman Amphitheatre

SAN FRANCESCO IN FIESOLE

To reach this, we leave Piazza del Duomo at Fiesole by Via San Francesco and climb up to the high point where once stood the Acropolis of the town (in the Classical period) which later became the medieval stronghold. The latter was replaced in 1330 by the present Church, at one time a Convent of the Hermit Nuns.

Interior: in the Gothic style, with interesting works of art;
The Crucifixion (Neri di Bicci) on the 2nd altar to the right
The Annunciation (Raffaellino) high altar
16th century inlaid choir-stalls in the apse
Madonna and Saints (Perugino) on the 2nd altar to the left.

From the **Sacristy,** to the left, we enter the **Large Cloister** (18th century) and from there go on to the **Museum of the Franciscan Missions.**

USEFUL INFORMATION FOR THE TOURIST

PUBLIC ASSISTANCE
(all cases of emergency) **Call. 113**

Other urgent telephone numbers:
Carabinieri (Flying squad) Phone 24444 - Central Police Station Phone 483201 - Police (Flying squad) Phone 55555 - Fire Brigade Phone 222222 - First Aid (Misericordia) Phone 27222 - Metropolitan Police Phone 496646 - Traffic Police Phone 43051.

Vital sentences:
I feel ill: **Mi sento male;**
My son is ill: **Mio figlio si sente male;**
My wife is ill: **Mia moglie si sente male.**
We need a doctor urgently: **Abbiamo bisogno urgentemente di un dottore;**
We need a dentist urgently: **abbiamo bisogno urgentemente di un dentista;**
We need an ambulance urgently: **abbiamo bisogno urgentemente di un'autoambulanza;**
Where is the nearest hospital?: **dov'è l'ospedale più vicino?**
Where is the nearest chemist's?: **dov'è la farmacia più vicina?**

Hospitals, all night surgery service:
S. Giovanni di Dio - Borgo Ognissanti 20, Phone 295444.
S. Maria Nuova - Piazza S. Maria Nuova, Phone 2774.

All Night Chemist's: Codecà, Via Ginori, 50 - Comunale, Via dei Serragli, 4 red - S. Maria Nuova, Piazza S. Maria Nuova, 1 red.

Turkish Baths: M. Caldi, Via Cavour, 19.
Beauty Parlours: Beauty Parlour, « Grazia », Por S. Maria, 6 - « Vivienne » - Piazza della Repubblica, 3.
Massages and Saunas: Istituto SFEM, Via Cavour, 108.
Pedicure: Freni, Piazza S. Lorenzo, 7 - Ida, Via Cerretani, 4.
Public Baths: Casa Poligrafici, Via dei Pepi, 28 - MI and RO, Via Porta Rossa, 23 - In the Station: Piazza della Stazione - « Centrale Bagni », Via de Pecori, 5.

Snack bars, cafeterias, etc: Giannino, Via Borgo S. Lorenzo - « Self-service », Via dei Peri, 5 - Grand Italia, Piazza della Stazione - Napoleone, Via dei Servi, 44.

Restaurants open till after midnight: Nuti, Via Borgo S. Lorenzo - La campana, Via Borgo S. Lorenzo - John Bull, Via Panzani - Buffet in the Station - La Bussola, Via di Porta Rossa, 58 red - Pizzeria Nannoni, Piazza Duomo, 27 red.

Restaurants with music and dancing: Giovacchino, Via Tosinghi - Open Gate, Via Michelangelo, 78.

Night clubs - Ballrooms: Moulin Rouge, Via Baccio Bandinelli, Phone 208608 - Open Gate, Via Michelangelo, 78 Phone 666398 - Roof Garden Baglioni, Piazza dell'Unità d'Italia, Phone 23846 - Chez Moi - Via di Porta Rossa, 15 - Phone 27232 - Pozzo di Beatrice, Piazza di S. Trinità, 5 red, Phone 270804.

Car-hire: AVIS, Borgognissanti, 134 red - Autosecci, Borgo S. Apostoli, 39 red - HERTZ, Via Maso Finiguerra, 33 red.
Real Estate Agencies: Giachetti, Piazza S. Maria Novella, 28 - S.T.A.C., Via dei Pucci, 9 - Piccioli, Piazza S. Giovanni, 5.

Petrol/gas coupon service: Automobil Club, Via Amendola, 36 - Foreign Visitors, Via Vecchietti, 22.
Petrol/gas stations always open: AGIP, Entry to Motorway - ESSO, Viale Europa, 225.

TOURIST ADDRESSES OF GENERAL INTEREST

Tourist Bodies:
— Azienda Autonoma di Turismo: Via Tornabuoni, 15 - tel. 276.544 - 276.545
— Ente Provinciale per il Turismo: Via Tornabuoni, 1 - telefoni 263.245/6/7

Tourist Guides:
— Ufficio Guide Turistiche - tel. 679.188

PALAZZO DEI CONGRESSI

— **Via Valfonda - Informazioni:**
— **Centro Internazionale Congressi**
— **50123 - Firenze**

Consulates:
— Belgio: Via de' Conti, 4 - tel. 294.276
— Danimarca: Via dei Servi, 13 - tel. 21.007
— Finlandia: Via Strozzi, 6 - tel. 260.831
— Francia: Piazza S. Trinità, 1 - tel. 23.509 - 298.966
— Germania: Borgo SS. Apostoli, 22 - tel. 294.722
— Gran Bretagna: Lungarno Corsini, 2 - tel. 284.133
— Norvegia: Via Sassetti, 4 - tel. 261.261
— Olanda: Via de' Conti, 4 - tel. 294.276
— Portogallo: Piazza Stazione, 1 - tel. 282.269
— San Marino: Via Roma, 3 - tel. 270.864
— Spagna: Via de' Conti, 4 - tel. 270.422
— Stati Uniti: Lungarno A. Vespucci, 38 - tel. 298.276/7
— Svezia: Via S. Reparata, 40 - tel. 496.692
— Svizzera: Via Tornabuoni, 1 - tel. 284.708 - 276.142

Airlines:
— Air France: Via Tornabuoni, 15 - tel. 263.208
— Alitalia: Lungarno Acciaioli 10/12r. - tel. 263.051/2/3
— B.E.A. - B.O.A.C. - Qantas - South African - Airways: Piazza Antinori, 5/7r. - tel. 283.749 - 287.405
— T.W.A.: Piazza Antinori, 2 - tel. 296.856 - 284.691

Italian Automobile Club - Via Amendola, 36 - Phone 674554.

Churches and Temples of the various religions:
Russian Orthodox - Via Leone X
Waldensian - Via Micheli (service in Italian)
Anglican (St. Marks Church) - Via Maggio, 16 (service in English)
Baptist - Via Borgognissanti, 6 (service in Italian)
Methodist - Via dei Benci, 9 (service in Italian)
American Episcopal - Via Rucellai, 15 (service in English)
Lutheran - Lungarno Torrigiani, (service in German)
Christian Science Church - Via della Spada, 1 (service in English)
Orthodox Apostolic Christian Catholic Church - Via Mannelli, 17
Lutheran Evangelic - Via de' Bardi, 20
Waldensian Evangelic of the Oratory - Via Manzoni, 21
Church of Nazarene - Via A. Miccinesi, 5 D
Israelic Temple - Via Farini, 4

GALLERIES - MUSEUMS - GARDENS (Hours)

Holidays 9 a.m. to 1 p.m. Entrance free	Summer	Winter	Entr. L.	Closed on
Galleria degli Uffizi - Logge Uffizi	10-16	10-16	250	Mondays
Galleria Palatina - Palazzo Pitti	10-16	10-16	200	Tuesdays
Museo degli Argenti - Palazzo Pitti	10-16	10-16	—	Tuesdays
Monumental Apartments - Palazzo Pitti				

	10-16	10-16	—	»
Galleria d'Arte Moderna - Palazzo Pitti	10-16	10-16	150	»
Galleria dell'Accademia - Via Ricasoli, 52	10-16	10-16	150	Mondays
Museo Nazionale (Bargello) Via Proconsolo, 4	10-16	10-16	150	Tuesdays
Raccolta della Ragione P.za Signoria	10-16	10-16		Tuesdays
Museo di S. Marco - Piazza S. Marco	10-16	10-16	150	Mondays
Museo della Casa Fiorentina Antica - Palazzo Davanzati	10-16	10-16	150	Mondays
Museo Archeologico - Piazza SS. Annunziata, 9	10-16	10-16	150	»
Casa Buonarotti - Via Ghibellina, 70	10-16	10-16	100	Tuesdays
Opificio delle Pietre Dure - Via Alfani, 78	Sundays	9.30-12.30	100	—
Cappelle Medicee (Michelangelo's tomb) - Piazza Madonna - S. Lorenzo	9- 17	9-16	200	—
Museo Fondazione Horne - Via dei Benci, 6	Mondays-Thursday		100	—
Giardino di Boboli - Piazza Pitti	9.00-6.30	9.30-4.30	—	—

GALLERIES & MUNICIPAL MUSEUMS: holidays 9.00-12.00

Palazzo Vecchio & Monumental Quarters - Piazza della Signoria	9-16	9-12	250	—
Galleria Corsi - Museo Berdini - Piazza de' Mozzi	9.00-4.00	9.00-4.00	100	Wednesday
Florence as it was - via dell'Oriolo, 24.	9.00-4.00	10.00-4.00	100	Thursday
Monumental Cloisters of S. Maria Novella	9.00-6.00	9.00-4.00	100	Friday
Cenacolo di S. Spirito	9.00-1.00	9.00-1.00	100	Mondays
Museo Stibbert - Via Stibbert, 26	9.00-4.00	9.00-4.000	200	—

OTHER MUSEUMS:

Galleria dello Spedale degli Innocenti	9.30-5.30		100	—
Museo dell'Opera di S. Croce - Piazza S. Croce	9.00-12.00	3.00-6.00	150	—
Museo dell'Opera del Duomo - Piazza Duomo, 9	9-1 & 3-6	9.30-5.00	150	—
Museo Antropologia & Etnologia - Open on request	Holidays	9.30-12.30	200	.—
Palazzo Medici Riccardi - Via Cavour, 1	9.00-1.00	3.00-5.30	100	..

MUSEUMS - VILLAS - MONUMENTS IN THE SURROUNDINGS

Belvedere Fortress (Free entrance to the square)
Fiesole - Bandini Museum: Entrance L. 100
Galluzzo - Certosa: Summertime 9-12 a.m. 2-6 p.m.: Wintertime
10-12 a.m. 2-5 p.m.
The entrance fees and the museum timetables may be changed.

Finito di stampare dalle Arti Grafiche Parigi & Maggiorelli, Firenze 1976